LSD

by David Petechuk

DRUG
EDUCATION
LIBRARY

LUCENT BOOKS

An imprint of Thomson Gale, a part of The Thomson Corporation

THOMSON

GALE

Detroit • New York • San Francisco • San Diego • New Haven, Conn.
Waterville, Maine • London • Munich

LIBRARY OF CONGRESS CATALOGING-IN-PUBLICATION DATA

Petechuk, David.
   LSD / by David Petechuk.
      p. cm. — (Drug education library)
   Includes bibliographical references and index.
   ISBN 1-59018-417-3 (hard cover : alk. paper)
   1. LSD—Juvenile literature. I. Title. II. Series.
   RM666.L88P48 2005
   615'.7883—dc22

                                                 2004010683

Printed in the United States of America

Contents

Foreword

The development of drugs and drug use in America is a cultural paradox. On the one hand, strong, potentially dangerous drugs provide people with relief from numerous physical and psychological ailments. Sedatives like Valium counter the effects of anxiety; steroids treat severe burns, anemia, and some forms of cancer; morphine provides quick pain relief. On the other hand, many drugs (sedatives, steroids, and morphine among them) are consistently misused or abused. Millions of Americans struggle each year with drug addictions that overpower their ability to think and act rationally. Researchers often link drug abuse to criminal activity, traffic accidents, domestic violence, and suicide.

These harmful effects seem obvious today. Newspaper articles, medical papers, and scientific studies have highlighted the myriad problems drugs and drug use can cause. Yet, there was a time when many of the drugs now known to be harmful were actually believed to be beneficial. Cocaine, for example, was once hailed as a great cure, used to treat everything from nausea and weakness to colds and asthma. Developed in Europe during the 1880s, cocaine spread quickly to the United States where manufacturers made it the primary ingredient in such everyday substances as cough medicines, lozenges, and tonics. Likewise, heroin, an opium derivative, became a popular painkiller during the late nineteenth century. Doctors and patients flocked to American drugstores to buy heroin, described as the optimal cure for even the worst coughs and chest pains.

As more people began using these drugs, though, doctors, legislators, and the public at large began to realize that they were more damaging than beneficial. After years of using heroin as a painkiller, for example, patients began asking their doctors for larger and stronger doses. Cocaine users reported dangerous side effects, including hallucinations and wild mood shifts. As a result, the U.S. government initiated more stringent regulation of many powerful and addictive drugs, and in some cases outlawed them entirely.

A drug's legal status is not always indicative of how dangerous it is, however. Some drugs known to have harmful effects can be purchased legally in the United States and elsewhere. Nicotine, a key ingredient in cigarettes, is known to be highly addictive. In an effort to meet their bodies' demands for nicotine, smokers expose themselves to lung cancer, emphysema, and other life-threatening conditions. Despite these risks, nicotine is legal almost everywhere.

Other drugs that cannot be purchased or sold legally are the subject of much debate regarding their effects on physical and mental health. Marijuana, sometimes described as a gateway drug that leads users to other drugs, cannot legally be used, grown, or sold in this country. However, some research suggests that marijuana is neither addictive nor a gateway drug and that it might actually benefit cancer and AIDS patients by reducing pain and encouraging failing appetites. Despite these findings and occasional legislative attempts to change the drug's status, marijuana remains illegal.

The Drug Education Library examines the paradox of drugs and drug use in America by focusing on some of the most commonly used and abused drugs or categories of drugs available today. By discussing objectively the many types of drugs, their intended purposes, their effects (both planned and unplanned), and the controversies surrounding them, the books in this series provide readers with an understanding of the complex role drugs and drug use play in American society. Informative sidebars, annotated bibliographies, and organizations to contact lists highlight the text and provide young readers with many opportunities for further discussion and research.

 **Introduction**

A Different and Mysterious Drug

Lysergic acid diethylamide (LSD) remains one of the most poorly understood and mysterious illegal drugs in the world, particularly because its effects are so intense and unpredictable. On one hand, some people report feelings of intense fear and paranoia while under its influence. They describe a descent into a hell on earth in which they became so afraid that they cowered in closets or checked themselves into a hospital for help. Others report feelings of happiness verging on euphoria. They claim to have attained keen insights into themselves and life.

Mysterious Effects

Often people taking LSD, or acid, face both the highs and the lows. One young user described his experience, often referred to as a trip, in this way: "As my acid trip went on, late at night, the good feelings started to shift to negative feelings. LSD intensified any negative feelings I had—if something was irritating me, the acid made it much worse."[1]

Because LSD can produce such wide-ranging and erratic effects, the drug's appeal is difficult for many people to understand. Its appeal also remains elusive because LSD alters basic processes.

As researchers Leigh A. Henderson and William J. Glass point out: "Our five senses are the tools we use to interpret the world. LSD alters the way these senses, particularly sight and hearing, function. Thus, like the sensation of an earthquake, LSD undermines the stability of the world as we know it."[2]

Another mysterious aspect of the drug is its ability to cause classic symptoms of psychoses. Sandoz Pharmaceuticals, which manufactured the drug at one time, and psychiatrists have pointed out that LSD causes symptoms of schizophrenia, like hallucinations and bizarre illusions. However, psychiatrists and others in the medical community believed LSD could be used to treat mental illnesses. Although the federal government has designated LSD as having no therapeutic value, some scientists assert that it has potential for treating psychiatric disorders and even addictions such as alcoholism. Few drugs with such unstable effects are considered in treatments.

Because LSD heightens sensory perception, some concertgoers, like these fans of The Grateful Dead, use the drug to enhance their appreciation of the music.

Most LSD users, like this one posing for a photo in 1968, come from solid middle- and upper-class backgrounds.

LSD also differs from most other known drugs, both legal and illegal, in that it appears to have few, if any, serious physical side effects. Almost any drug can have adverse effects on the body. Smoke from marijuana, for example, can harm the lungs. The legal drug aspirin can cause bleeding ulcers. Although scientists argue about whether LSD has long-term effects on the mind, most agree that its physical effects are relatively benign. This does not mean that LSD cannot adversely affect a person. Many people who have used LSD repeatedly over time have reported difficulties in learning, sleeping, and declining intellectual performance.

Users and Dealers

Still another confounding aspect of LSD relates to its users. Although all kinds of people use drugs illegally, illegal drug abuse is generally associated with people who are less educated and poor. Typical LSD users, however, are people who come from solid middle- and upper-class backgrounds and have many opportunities to pursue a higher education and successful careers. Studies of LSD users, especially those from the 1960s and 1970s, have shown that many of them are intelligent.

Even the illegal trafficking and sale of LSD does not follow the norm. Law enforcement agencies, including the U.S. Drug Enforcement Administration (DEA), have recognized that they are targeting a different type of drug dealer. For one thing, the DEA has noted that profit often does not seem to be the primary motivating factor in LSD sales. It appears that dealers are more interested in sharing the LSD experience with others. According to the DEA, "Their belief in the beneficent properties of LSD has been, over the years, as strong a motivating factor in the production and distribution of the drug as the profits to be made from its sale."[3]

The Mysteries Remain

Many questions about LSD remain unanswered. Whether it has serious long-term effects on the mind and whether it can be developed for therapeutic use are issues that continue to be debated. Some scientists even wonder if studies of LSD's effects on the mind can shed light on how the mind functions and influences human behavior. Because LSD research has been greatly restricted, many of these questions may remain unanswered.

Despite the many debates about LSD among the medical community, one thing is known and generally agreed upon: LSD is a drug with potential dangers and should not be used recreationally. As stated in *Current Health*, LSD can have frightening effects: "No one can predict if an LSD trip will be good or bad. LSD can cause terrifying thoughts and feelings and fear of insanity and death."[4] This possibility contributed to the federal government classifying LSD as an illegal drug with no known benefits.

Chapter 1

LSD's Origins

L SD is the most potent hallucinogen known to science. Consuming an amount in weight equal to a few grains of salt can produce wide-ranging effects, including rich and vivid hallucinations and visions. The effects of LSD often vary from person to person, and the intensity of the effects depends on how much of the drug is taken.

What Is LSD?

LSD is often classified as a synthetic drug because it is produced only in a laboratory. Although most hallucinogenic drugs, such as marijuana and peyote, come from plants, LSD is not derived completely from a natural biological source, that is, a plant or an animal. LSD is more accurately called a semisynthetic hallucinogen because it has both natural and synthetic components.

Diethylamide is LSD's synthetic ingredient. It is part of a group of chemical compounds called amides. Diethylamide and other amides are used in drugs because of their ability to bond with molecules in the body, primarily proteins. In the case of LSD, diethylamide allows LSD to bond with certain molecules in the brain, helping the body to process the drug. LSD's hallucinogenic ef-

fects, however, come from lysergic acid, which is found in morning glory seeds and more commonly in an ergot fungus called
Clavica pupurea that grows on rye and certain other grains. The

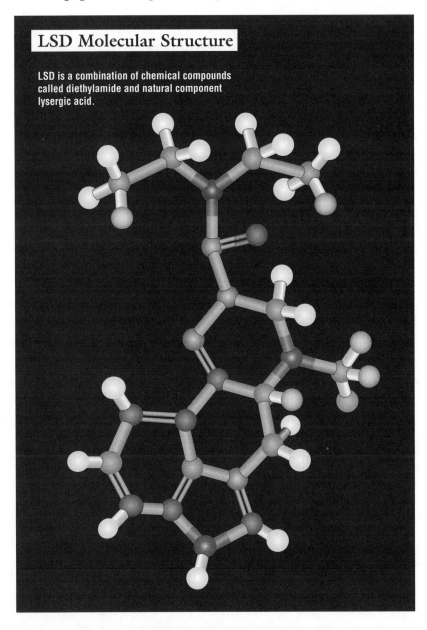

LSD Molecular Structure

LSD is a combination of chemical compounds
called diethylamide and natural component
lysergic acid.

lysergic acid is derived from a substance in the fungus that is used to make many drugs, including effective medicines for treating migraine headaches.

How Was LSD Discovered?

LSD was discovered in the 1930s as a result of research at Sandoz Pharmaceuticals in Switzerland into possible medical uses for the ergot fungus. Scientists at the Rockefeller Institute in New York had isolated a chemical compound found in the ergot fungus and named it lysergic acid. A young chemist at Sandoz named Albert Hofmann began working with lysergic acid derivatives. He was trying to develop a strong stimulant that would act on the human respiratory and circulatory systems and help breathing for people who had respiratory diseases or suffered from respiratory failure. In 1938 Hofmann synthesized lysergic acid diethylamide and gave it the lab name LSD-25 because it was the twenty-fifth compound

The seeds of the morning glory plant contain lysergic acid, the hallucinogenic component of LSD.

he synthesized in his series of experiments. (The abbreviation LSD comes from the drug's German name, *lyserg saeure diathylamid*.)

Sandoz researchers tested LSD-25 in animals and concluded that the drug held little promise for medical use. Hofmann halted his research but returned to studying LSD five years later, in 1943. After resuming his investigations, Hofmann accidentally contaminated himself with the drug. Although he was not sure exactly how the contamination occurred, Hofmann believed he had absorbed it through the skin of his fingertips during the laboratory process of producing a crystallized form of LSD. Before long Hofmann began to feel a strange sense of restlessness and dizziness, and he decided to go home to rest. In his 1980 book *LSD: My Problem Child*, Hofmann described his experience this way:

> At home I lay down and sank into a not unpleasant intoxicated-like condition, characterized by an extremely stimulated imagination. In a dreamlike state, with eyes closed (I found the daylight to be unpleasantly glaring), I perceived an uninterrupted stream of fantastic pictures, extraordinary shapes with intense, kaleidoscopic play of colors. After some two hours this condition faded away.[5]

Hofmann believed the experience was related to his experiments. Intrigued, he intentionally took LSD-25 three days later. Hofmann took only 0.25 milligrams of the substance, which is a very small dose compared to the dosages required for most drugs to have an effect. He again experienced a variety of unusual sensory experiences, some horrifying and others pleasant. The experience confirmed that LSD-25 had a powerful effect on humans.

LSD's Potency

LSD is extremely potent. The amount needed to produce an effect is measured in mere micrograms. A microgram is equal to about one-millionth (1/1,000,000) of a gram. In comparison, dosages of most drugs are measured in milligrams, with one milligram equaling about one-thousandth (1/1,000) of a gram. According to the DEA, LSD is so potent that one gram of the powder form of LSD could be sold as twenty thousand individual units.

Scientific Names for LSD and Hallucinogens

The original term for the class of drugs now called hallucinogens was *phantastica*. This scientific term was created by a renowned pharmacologist and toxicologist named Louis Lewin in his 1924 book *Phantastica*. The book is considered a classic study on the use of drugs that affect the mind, mood, or other mental processes. Based largely on research with LSD, the psychiatric community later named hallucinogens *psychotomimetics* or *psychosomimetics*, meaning that people taking them sometimes act as though they have a true psychosis, such as paranoia and schizophrenia.

In the 1960s Humphrey Osmond, a British psychiatrist who worked with LSD as a therapy for alcoholics and schizophrenics, came up with the term that would apply to LSD and all other hallucinogens. Convinced that mimicking mental illness was not the main characteristic of LSD, Osmond suggested that the group of drugs be called *psychedelic*, which means "mind-manifesting." Following this line of thought, scholars created the name *entheogen* in 1979. The word *entheogen* comes from the Greek word *entheos*, meaning "god within" and the Greek root *gen*, which denotes the act of becoming. Thus, *entheogen* can be translated as "producing the divine within." This name reflects the spiritual and mystical experiences many people have claimed to experience while taking LSD and other hallucinogens.

The dosage of LSD needed to produce a hallucinogenic effect depends, in part, on a person's body weight. For example, a dosage of only 17.5 micrograms can produce mild effects in a person who weighs approximately 155 pounds but can cause more noticeable effects in someone who weighs less. In general, LSD dosages begin at 25 micrograms, and the average oral dose of LSD is 50 to 100 micrograms.

The strength of LSD dosages varies widely, however, and cannot be guaranteed. The Food and Drug Administration (FDA) regulates legal drugs. In addition to conducting a thorough review and approval process to determine a drug's safety, the FDA monitors and approves a legal drug's contents and establishes manufacturing standards for making the drug. Because manufacturing LSD is illegal and unregulated, its users have no practical way of determining exactly how much LSD they are taking.

Another problem associated with LSD is its unknown purity. Laboratory tests have revealed some LSD to be mixed with other drugs or substances, including phencyclidine (PCP) and amphetamines. These drugs can have serious side effects. For example, high dosages of PCP can cause seizures, respiratory failure, stroke, and heart problems. Amphetamines can also cause heart problems and even lead to heart attacks. At one time, many believed that strychnine, which is a rat poison, was used to manufacture LSD. Although strychnine was once found in a batch of LSD when it began to be illegally manufactured more than three decades ago, large-scale lab analyses of street samples have failed to find strychnine in LSD. Nevertheless, the bottom line is that any unregulated drug, such as LSD, may include other potentially harmful drugs.

LSD Comes in Various Forms

Making LSD is a complex chemical process that requires sophisticated lab equipment and an experienced organic chemist. Although

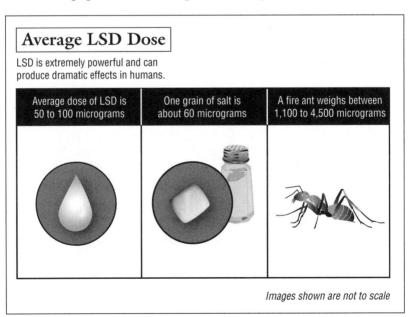

Average LSD Dose

LSD is extremely powerful and can produce dramatic effects in humans.

Average dose of LSD is 50 to 100 micrograms	One grain of salt is about 60 micrograms	A fire ant weighs between 1,100 to 4,500 micrograms

Images shown are not to scale

the resulting synthesized product is a crystallized white, odorless powder, LSD is seldom seen in the crystal form. Rather, the powder, which is water soluble, is diluted and distributed in other forms.

As a liquid, LSD may be dropped directly in the mouth. It can also be ingested orally by either sucking on sugar cubes containing LSD or swallowing extremely small tablets of LSD called "microdots." One of the most popular forms of illegal LSD is "blotter," that is, small squares of paper that have been soaked in liquid LSD. Another form of LSD is small, clear gelatin squares, which are known as "windowpanes" or "gel tabs."

LSD is most often taken orally. However, it can be inhaled through the nose in powder form and injected intravenously via a needle. Because the drug is so powerful, few people take LSD in these ways.

How Does LSD Work?

After taking LSD, a person experiences its effects within thirty to ninety minutes. Several factors can influence how quickly the drug is absorbed. For example, it takes longer to affect someone who has eaten a big meal as opposed to someone who ingests LSD on an empty stomach. The effects continue for six to twelve hours.

Blotter Acid

Although LSD comes in several forms, the paper form, called blotter acid, is the most common way LSD is sold on the streets. Blotter is made when an absorbent paper is soaked and diluted in LSD. The amount of acid diluted into the paper can vary greatly, depending on the batch. This means it is difficult for someone taking the illegal drug to know the strength of the dose or the powerful effects that will be experienced. The paper sheets are also perforated so that individual "tabs" can be sold or taken. These tabs are extremely small because it takes only a small dose of LSD to produce its effects. Blotter LSD is also often imprinted with some type of art, such as cartoon characters like Bart Simpson and Daffy Duck, or other designs, such as flowers or rainbows.

Once LSD is ingested, it is absorbed rapidly from the stomach and intestines into the bloodstream, where it is distributed throughout the body's many tissues. Although LSD's exact mechanism of action is unknown, scientists believe that it stimulates certain brain cells to produce its effects.

LSD and Serotonin

In the brain, nerve cells called neurons use a variety of chemical molecules called neurotransmitters to send signals to each other. Between each neuron is a small gap called the synapse. Neurotransmitters are released from one neuron and then cross the synapse, where they may be accepted by the next neuron at a special site called a receptor. The neurotransmitter carries nerve impulses across the synapse, helping to relay various messages to different parts of the brain. There are many different types of neurotransmitters in the brain. Some play a large role in many of our sensory and emotional responses, including hunger, thirst, pleasure, and pain.

In the case of LSD, scientists believe that the drug interferes with a neurotransmitter called serotonin. This interference occurs because the molecular structures of LSD and serotonin are very similar. As a result, LSD is believed to interfere with serotonin's normal action at the receptor sites of some neurons.

Serotonin helps regulate behavior and normal body functions. For example, changes in serotonin production in the brain can affect mood, sleep, and appetite. Scientists also know that lowered levels of serotonin in the brain play a key role in causing depression in some people. Because LSD affects serotonin in the brain, someone under the influence of LSD may experience various changes in their moods and emotions, such as depression or euphoria.

Due to LSD's interference with serotonin, LSD may work as a pain reliever, or analgesic. Scientists believe this effect occurs because most serotonin neurons are located in the middle of the brain stem, which is involved in the regulation of pain. As a result, LSD may somehow interfere with the transfer of pain messages across neurons.

What Are LSD's Effects?

Clearly, LSD affects the brain in many ways. The most important aspects of LSD are its psychological and sensory effects. For example, scientists know that LSD primarily affects neurons that play a large role in people's perceptions and various other mental processes, including awareness and judgment.

Someone taking LSD often experiences an intensified perception of colors, smells, sounds, and other sensations. Sometimes the sensations become mixed, which is a phenomenon called synesthesia. As a result, a person may believe he or she can hear or feel colors and taste sounds. Many scientists believe that this phenomenon is due to LSD's effects on a part of the brain called the

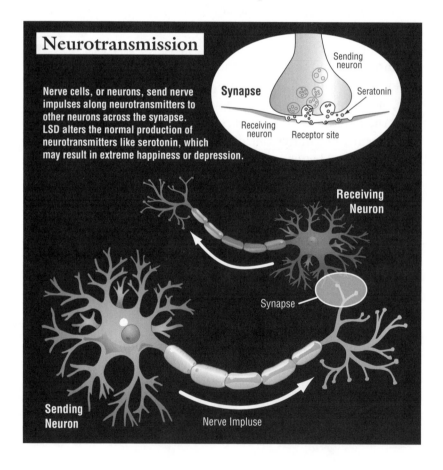

Neurotransmission

Nerve cells, or neurons, send nerve impulses along neurotransmitters to other neurons across the synapse. LSD alters the normal production of neurotransmitters like serotonin, which may result in extreme happiness or depression.

Synapse

Sending neuron

Seratonin

Receiving neuron

Receptor site

Receiving Neuron

Synapse

Sending Neuron

Nerve Impulse

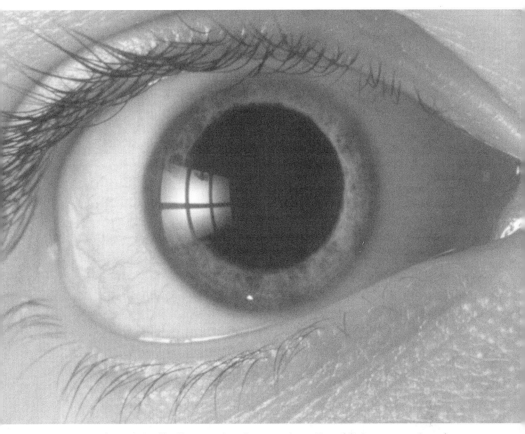

LSD dramatically distorts visual perception. In addition to causing the pupil to dilate, the drug produces intense visual illusions.

locus coeruleus, which helps to interpret sound, touch, smell, and taste. Because sensory perceptions are greatly altered, the LSD user often experiences time as slowing down.

LSD also affects areas of the brain dealing with vision. As well as causing the physical dilation of pupils, LSD distorts electrical messages sent to and from various parts of the brain that regulate and interpret visual information. As a result, a common effect of LSD are visual illusions that distort or transform shapes and movements. Visual illusions may include intensified color, flashing lights, and brightly colored geometric designs.

In addition to causing visual and perceptual distortions, LSD has other temporary physiological effects. It can increase a person's blood pressure and heart rate and cause nausea, increased salivation, tremors, and muscle weakness. Dry mouth, sweating, and loss of appetite can also occur, as can tingling and numbness of the skin.

Tolerance

Although the effects produced by LSD can be extreme and unpleasant, some people continue to use the drug. When a drug or substance is used over and over again, a condition known as tolerance can occur.

Tolerance is a state in which a person's body adjusts to repeatedly taking a drug. As a result, the person becomes less responsive to the drug's physical or mental effects. The more tolerant someone becomes to a drug, the weaker the effect of a single dose on that person. As a result, the person may take more of the drug to obtain the desired effect, whether it is to eliminate pain or to produce intoxication, the feeling of being "high."

LSD users develop a rapid tolerance to the drug's effects. As a result, users must take larger quantities of the drug in order to experience its effects. However, the drug cannot be abused for more than a few consecutive days. After that, it will not produce hallucinogenic effects, no matter how much is taken. In most cases, if someone stops taking LSD for several days to a week, the tolerance wears off rapidly.

Is LSD Addictive?

Repeatedly taking any drug, whether legal or illegal, often leads to addiction, a condition in which a user experiences abnormally strong physical or psychological cravings for the drug. A physical addiction occurs when the body adapts and becomes used to the presence of the drug. The physical addiction can be so strong that eventually the body cannot function normally without the drug. For example, a person addicted to drugs like alcohol or heroin may experience shaking, nausea, insomnia, diarrhea, and vomiting

Medics use a stretcher to carry an overdose victim from a 1975 concert. Although fatal overdoses of LSD are rare, long-term use of the drug can cause lasting physical harm.

when they go without taking the drug. These conditions are commonly referred to as withdrawal symptoms and often occur when the drug use is reduced or stopped abruptly.

Both scientists and law enforcement officials agree that LSD is not a physically addictive drug. It does not result in the user having an uncontrollable need to seek out the drug, which often occurs with the use of other drugs. Even with chronic use over a long period of time, LSD produces no physical withdrawal symptoms.

Does LSD Cause Psychological Dependency?

LSD use can lead to a psychological dependency or addiction in some people. Users may not experience physical withdrawal but may feel they must take the drug to escape from reality, forget about their problems, or relieve feelings of loneliness and anxiety. People who believe that they need the drug to improve their mood can become dependent on the euphoric feelings that the drug gives them.

The consensus, though, is that LSD does not have a high potential for psychological dependency. Regarding the recreational use of LSD, a DEA report noted, "Several factors provide LSD with a virtually inherent governor to its regular use, meaning that the drug will never become as frequently abused as other drugs, most notably, crack cocaine." According to the DEA report, the long duration of the drug's effects means that most people will not purchase or take the drug on a rapidly recurring basis. The DEA also noted that the drug's uncertain effects lead most people to discontinue its use. The report concluded, "Finally, the extremely powerful and intense hallucinations often prompt users to abstain from LSD ingestion as they require periods of reorientation."[6]

LSD and Overdosing

People who take drugs run the risk of overdose. Taking an excessive amount of a drug often has toxic or lethal effects. According to the DEA, it is virtually impossible to die from an overdose of LSD. Whereas a lethal dose of LSD is considered to be 12,000 micrograms, based on tests in which this dosage killed 50 percent of the animals tested, humans generally take 100 micrograms. Only two human deaths from the physiological effects of LSD have been reported in medical literature. In both cases, doctors found that the individuals had a large amount of LSD in the liver and no other drug. One of the deaths occurred in a hospital and was due to a malfunction in the respiratory system that made the person quit breathing.

Rare instances of fatal overdose highlight the fact that all drugs have the potential to be fatal. Even if it does not cause death, LSD taken in large amounts can physically harm people. In a case reported in *Clinical Toxicology* in 1975, eight people at a party mistook crystal LSD for cocaine and inhaled a large quantity of the drug. As a result, the individuals experienced vomiting and collapsed. They were rushed to the hospital, where doctors found that they were suffering from symptoms of hyperthermia (high fever) and respiratory problems. Such cases are rare in that few users have access to large quantities of LSD, but they demonstrate the drug's dangers, nonetheless.

Can LSD Harm the Brain?

The long-term use of most drugs can have a profound impact on a person's body and overall health. Heavy alcohol use, for instance, can damage and ultimately destroy a person's liver. It has been well documented that many prescription drugs have harmful and even fatal side effects. On the other hand, the damage LSD causes to the body is highly debated.

Scientists have not been able to prove, for example, whether LSD permanently damages brain tissues and functioning. Some researchers have reported that LSD users experience permanent cerebral deficits, that is, problems within the brain that affect how

The Fires of Saint Anthony

In his book *The Day of St. Anthony's Fire*, author John G. Fuller tells the true and tragic story of the people in a small French village, Pont-Saint-Esprit, who appeared to go insane. In mid-August 1951, some villagers began running through the streets, screaming that wild animals and bandits were chasing them. Others did not sleep for days and walked around having pleasant and sometimes spiritual visions or delusions. A few citizens thought they could fly and jumped from their second-story windows into the Rhone River.

Scientific investigations eventually uncovered the culprit. The villagers had been poisoned by the wheat and rye flour fungus called ergot. LSD is synthetically developed from this fungus. A local baker had used the contaminated flour to bake bread. Overall some 230 villagers, all customers of the baker, suffered from ergot poisoning, which is now known as ergotism. In medieval times, ergot poisoning was called St. Anthony's fire after the medieval patron saint and the Order of St. Anthony members who provided care for those stricken with the mysterious disease.

it functions. Electroencephalograms (EEGs) are recordings of electrical activity within the brain. Abnormal brain wave patterns have been detected in the EEGs of some people who have taken LSD over a period of time. However, the results are inconclusive and lack statistical data.

Although no concrete evidence is available, scientists and physicians remain concerned that LSD may cause irreversible changes in the brain. What they know for certain is that some people who have taken LSD over a period of time show signs of mental or cognitive impairment, such as learning and memory problems, while others appear to function normally. The inconclusive data on the long-term effects of LSD use was described in the *American Journal of Psychiatry* in 1969 and pertains today: "In one subject who continued to use the drug heavily, there was a deterioration in his performance pattern on the cognitive tests suggestive of organic [physical] damage. On the other hand one of our subjects maintained an A average in junior college while ingesting LSD on most weekends."[7]

Does LSD Cause Chromosome Damage?

One of the earliest reports concerning LSD's potential to cause physical harm focused on chromosome damage in users. A 1967 study by Dr. Marion Cohen of the State University of New York at Buffalo reported that LSD damaged white-blood-cell chromosomes in test tubes. Chromosomes, found in the cell nucleus, contain most of the chemicals, called DNA and RNA, that are responsible for an individual's genetic makeup. Because chromosomes carry the genetic codes for life from generation to generation, chromosome damage can lead to abnormalities in unborn children.

Cohen's report set off a firestorm of controversy. The authors of a *Consumer Reports* article noted, "Reporters (and physicians as well) speculated in print and on television and radio that LSD might cause a vast epidemic of tragically malformed babies."[8]

When researchers pursued this avenue of investigation, their results were contradictory and inconclusive. Studies focused on animal subjects, and extremely high doses (up to 500,000 milligrams) of LSD were given early in the pregnancy of some animals. In his *American Journal of Psychiatry* article that reviewed follow-up research into chromosome damage, psychologist B. Kent Houston noted, "Even at this high a dosage, there was no evidence that LSD led to an unusual frequency of mutations."[9] LSD usage cannot be pinpointed as a cause of chromosomal damage because scientists point out that breakage can occur as a response to a variety of factors, including many pollutants, X rays, fever, and even a viral infection. Evidence has shown that even aspirin and caffeine may cause chromosome damage in some cells.

Does LSD Cause Damage to the Embryo?

Several reports have indicated that women who take LSD just prior to or during pregnancy increase their risk of having a miscarriage or stillbirth. Once again, the research has been inconclusive, because scientists cannot trace the miscarriages directly to LSD consumption. For example, in almost all the cases studied, the mothers had taken other drugs during pregnancy, a circumstance that makes it difficult to determine whether LSD, another drug, or a combination of drugs and other factors contributed to problems.

In the 2001 book *Drugs in Pregnancy and Lactation*, Gerald G. Briggs and his coeditors noted that a direct relationship between LSD dosage and miscarriages could not be established. They further concluded that no study had confirmed that LSD causes chromosome damage or an increased rate of miscarriage and that more research is needed.

Because LSD's effects on the embryo and unborn child are undetermined, physicians recommend that women avoid taking the drug during pregnancy, especially since LSD enters into the placenta easily. Health professionals agree that even the remote possibility of chromosome or fetal damage in humans requires that women who are either pregnant or expect to become pregnant in the near future avoid LSD use.

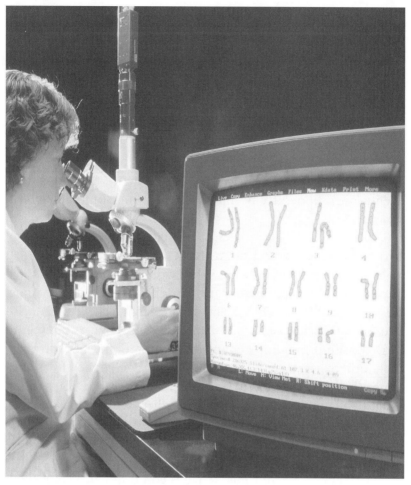

Recent studies have demonstrated that LSD use does not cause chromosomal damage as previously believed.

Although controversy continues to surround LSD's potentially harmful effects on the body, scientists have documented its profound long- and short-term psychological impact. As a result, a clearer picture of how LSD affects the mind has emerged.

Chapter 2

LSD and the Mind

How LSD affects a person's mind can vary widely. Many people who have taken LSD claim it is a mind-expanding drug that produces feelings of euphoria or intense happiness while increasing awareness and understanding of life. Others feel quite the contrary and have reported experiencing extremely negative emotions such as fear and anxiety and overall unpleasant experiences.

Clearly, the LSD user's experience is characterized by heightened feelings and emotions. In an article in *Process Studies*, Dr. Leonard Gibson noted that, whether the experience is good or bad, "everything seems to take on deeper significance, a myriad of meaning unlock in each individual thing. Events brim over with significance."[10]

Since the 1960s, the broad experiences produced by LSD have been called a "trip," like "drunk" is used to describe the overall effects of alcohol. The term comes from LSD's long duration in the body, which can typically last up to twelve hours. It also relates to the powerful mental experience people have while under the influence of LSD, which includes a drastic change in their overall perception of the world. In this sense, the LSD user has taken a trip to another world. Beyond these basics, no two trips are exactly the same.

Hallucinations

The most notable features of a trip are the sensory and perceptual changes a person experiences. In addition to visual disturbances such as flashing colors, LSD often produces visions or illusions that appear to be real. While the overall hallucinations may seem unbelievable, these visions are usually based on something real. For example, an LSD user could believe she is having a conversation with her pet. According to researcher Leigh A. Henderson, "LSD alters the way in which existing sensory stimuli are perceived, and the user typically remains aware that his or her perceptions are drug induced."[11]

In a 1966 *Life* magazine article about LSD, the editors put it this way: "A stick may become a writhing snake . . . and though the person may be frightened by the snake, he realizes that it is not a real snake but an illusory one."[12]

The illusions resulting from LSD use vary depending on the dosage. The DEA notes:

> Initially, at lower dosage levels, the visual images are intensified in color or flashes of light are seen. The visual images progress to brightly colored geometric designs and become distorted. At higher dosages, images appear as distortions of reality or as completely new visual images and can be seen with the eyes open or closed.[13]

LSD Affects How a Person Feels

In addition to producing visual illusions, LSD makes a person feel different. A common experience during LSD trips is feeling detached from the body, also known as depersonalization. Some people even experience a sense of levitation, that is, the feeling that the body is rising from the ground or floating. Some describe the experience as feeling that their bodies do not belong to them or that they are standing beside themselves. Leigh A. Henderson reports, "It is often described as a feeling that the mind is transcending the boundaries of the individual self."[14]

The feeling of depersonalization also often involves a temporary loss of the user's sense of self as a distinct individual. Henderson notes, "Users may temporarily lose their sense of identity, but

A woman on LSD examines a statue during a 1963 experiment. High dosages of LSD can produce very powerful and believable hallucinations.

The September 9, 1966, edition of Life *magazine featured art created under the effects of LSD.*

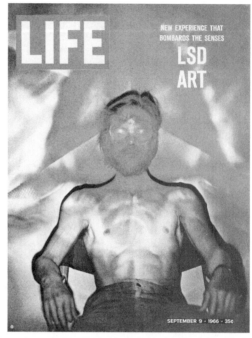

they are usually not delirious. Thoughts are dreamlike, flowing freely; short-term memory and abstract reasoning are impaired."[15]

Likewise, author William Braden describes one of the hallmarks of the experience as the loss of ego or sense of self. Braden notes, "Awareness of individual identity evaporates. 'I' and 'me' are no more." He goes on to describe the feeling of some LSD users that they are no longer separate from the things around them but are a part of evertything: "Subject-object relationships dissolve, and . . . the world is simply an extension of the body."[16]

Consciousness Expanding Experiences

Many LSD users have reported reaching new states of conscious-ness or awareness in which they believe they have experienced great insights. The LSD user may believe that he or she has a new and complete understanding of life and its meaning. "The subject feels he knows, essentially, everything there is to know," Braden writes. "He knows ultimate truth."[17] LSD users have described these expe-riences as cosmic, transcendental, religious, or mystical in nature.

Ultimately, the experience is intensely personal. Whether or not it is mystical or religious depends on how the individual interprets the experience. In other words, the drug itself does not produce the feeling that someone is experiencing something beyond the ordinary realm of human experience, but it does open the door to that realm. As noted by early LSD researchers Timothy Leary, Ralph Metzner, and Richard Alpert in their book *The Psychedelic Experience*, LSD "merely acts as a chemical key—it opens the mind, frees the nervous system of its ordinary patterns and structures."[18]

LSD and Creativity

Many have contended that LSD can help a person achieve new levels of insight, problem solving, spontaneity, and creativity. Others argue that such beliefs are difficult to assess and nearly impossible to prove. Overall, studies of creativity have produced conflicting results.

In a study published in *Psychosomatics* in 1971, researcher G.J. Sarwer Foner came to the conclusion that LSD does not enhance creativity. Dr. Oscar Janiger and Marlene Dobkin de Rios came to a different conclusion in their article "LSD and Creativity," published in 1989 in the *Journal of Psychoactive Drugs*. Based on clinical studies of LSD that took place between 1954 and 1962, the authors reported that LSD could enhance creativity as well as appreciation of the arts and beauty. In the authors' 2003 book, *LSD, Spirituality, and the Creative Process*, several artists discussed their experience of trying to create while under the influence of LSD. Janiger and Dobkin de Rios noted, "Overall, the artists reported that in their LSD experiences they had gained the ability to generate original insights, fresh perspectives and novel, creative form." Janiger and Dobkin de Rios stressed that LSD-inspired artwork is not necessarily "superior to those performed in ordinary states of consciousness."

Most scientists agree that it is difficult, if not impossible, to develop meaningful tests for proving whether LSD can enhance a person's creativity and performance. In its report "LSD," the Canadian Government Commission of Inquiry noted, "Although sophisticated scientific investigation in this area is only just beginning, it is already obvious that LSD will not perform the miracle of turning an uninspired and untalented individual into a creative genius. The question of more subtle effects on creative activity in certain individuals must be answered by future research."

Changing Moods and Feelings

Studies have shown that the moods of someone taking LSD can change quickly and profoundly. In a matter of seconds, a person may go from extreme excitability to a feeling of tranquility.

As with many drugs, a person's own psychological makeup and current mood combined with environmental factors play key roles in LSD's ultimate psychological effects. For example, if someone is mildly depressed or anxious before taking LSD, the drug can enhance and intensify these feelings. If someone on LSD encounters a threatening or unpleasant situation, or is in an unfamiliar environment, he or she may experience intense feelings of fear or paranoia, sometimes beyond the point of control. As noted in a report on LSD by the Canadian Government Commission:

> The psychological effects of LSD are not readily predictable and are determined to a considerable degree by various personality factors in the individual, his past history and experiences, his attitudes and expectations, and motivations, the general setting in which the drug is taken, persons accompanying the "trip" and external events occurring during the experience.[19]

What Is a Bad Trip?

Although on a good trip LSD users may feel they have attained great insights, these insights may quickly become terrifying. Most often, a bad trip is described as an acute anxiety or panic reaction that lasts for an extended period of time, a couple of hours or more. In addition to feelings of panic and anxiety, someone on a bad trip may experience a wide range of negative emotions. In the *Journal of Nervous and Mental Diseases*, author Rick Strassman sums up the overall symptoms of a bad trip as possibly including "frightening illusions/hallucinations (usually visual and/or auditory); overwhelming anxiety to the point of panic; aggression with possible violent acting-out behavior; depression with suicidal ideations, gestures, or attempts; confusion; and fearfulness to the point of paranoid delusions."[20]

A bad trip may also be characterized as feeling a loss of control. LSD users may feel helpless to control their emotions. For example, they may begin laughing or crying uncontrollably or become

During a bad trip, LSD users may experience frightening hallucinations that can cause lasting trauma.

suspicious of everyone, even their parents or friends. The loss of control usually occurs when users begin to believe that their hallucinations are real or become unable to respond appropriately to situations. Scientists James MacDonald and Michael Agar discuss these two ways in which LSD users spin out of control:

> The first is to lose the knowledge that the distortions are not real. The trip changes from an alternative reality to the only reality; one starts to think it will never end. The second way to lose control, even if one maintains the knowledge that the distortions are not real, is to lose control of the actual situation. The situation makes demands that cannot be met; circumstances require a level of awareness and directed response that is made impossible by the LSD. One believes oneself to be in serious trouble, but cannot understand what is happening well enough to react appropriately.[21]

Stopping a Bad Trip

These feelings of fear sometimes escalate to the point at which users fear that they are insane or that they may never return to a normal state of mind. Most people who have a bad trip can be calmed down by reassurances that the experience is only temporary and will end once the drug wears off. However, some people do not respond to reassurances and end up going to the hospital when, for example, they cannot control an intense panic reaction.

Once in the hospital, the doctor usually keeps the patient in a quiet room free from disturbing outside influences, including anxious friends. The physician or nurse reassures the patient that the mind or brain is not permanently damaged. They also let the patient know that the effects of the drug will gradually wear off. Sometimes a calm, supportive friend or relative stays with the patient if the physician or nurse must leave. If the patient continues to be highly agitated, drugs like diazepam (Valium) and chlorpromazine (Thorazine) may be given to calm him or her down. Patients are usually not strapped down or restrained because such treatment may worsen their anxiety and paranoia. The hospital staff, however, usually take measures, such as keep-

---

A Bad Trip

In the book *LSD: Still with Us After All These Years*, contributors James MacDonald and Michael Agar interviewed several young people who had taken LSD. MacDonald and Agar noted that "sometimes users have bad trips that reach nightmarish proportions." One user described such a trip in which he witnessed a fight and thought his life was in danger. He described his reactions this way:

> I freaked out, put myself in a closet. I strictly lost it—I landed outside a couple of times you know, ran in the woods, got lost in the woods. . . . My feeling was like, "This is never going to stop," you know. I had no sensation of, like, that this was slowing down at all. Once it started, it was like I was peaking forever. It started, you know, hanging upside down, I was just like all clenched up, all sweaty, my hat was completely wet. . . . The feeling was just shaky and there was so much tension it was just scary, it was like so emotional. There was just too much emotion involved, and it was a really scary experience.

ing sharp objects out of the patient's reach, to prevent him or her from causing harm to oneself or others.

Before a patient on a bad trip can leave the hospital, a psychiatrist usually examines them to determine whether or not he or she has returned to a normal mental state. If the patient has returned to normal, they are released. In rare cases, the patient may be kept in the hospital if suicidal or psychotic tendencies persist.

Dangerous Accidents

Keeping an eye on users is important because LSD greatly affects how they perceive themselves and the world around them. Sometimes, LSD use can lead to foolish or irrational behavior, such as the users thinking they can fly or that they are indestructible. Some experts believe that such thoughts have led some users to jump off buildings or attempt other dangerous stunts. Users may unintentionally harm themselves in other ways. For example, in the early 1970s many reports circulated that LSD users were going blind from staring at the sun without blinking for several minutes. Although no one was actually blinded, a dozen cases of people on LSD harming their retinas from gazing at the sun were reported in national newspapers. Some believe these reports were a hoax, however.

In addition, overall functioning is often greatly impaired while using LSD because sensory input, such as sights and sounds, is often warped and difficult to interpret. As a result, the LSD user is more likely to make misjudgments and become involved in accidents. For example, driving a car and even walking in some cases can be extremely dangerous because of visual stimuli, like flashing or bright lights, that are distracting and increase the potential for critical misjudgments.

Does LSD Cause Self-Destructive or Violent Behavior?

In addition to accidents, concerns have been raised about the connection between LSD use and other self-destructive behavior. Several attempts at self-mutilation have been reported in LSD users, but none of these have been documented. In a few cases, people who have taken LSD have become depressed and attempted suicide.

Drug use is often associated with violent behaviors. For example, people drunk on alcohol can be violent, as evidenced by bar fights and an association between spousal abuse and alcoholism. For the most part, reports of users becoming violent while under the influence of LSD are rare. Police have reported that people who were high on LSD committed several homicides, but none of these reports have been well documented. Commenting on a handful of homicide cases associated with LSD use that were reported in a 1969 article, Leigh A. Henderson notes, "Aggression is not a common response to LSD . . . and the involvement of other drugs, and, particularly, prior psychiatric illness appear to have been contributing factors."[22]

Does LSD Cause Psychosis?

Although most negative reactions end after the effects of LSD wear off, there are concerns that LSD use can cause long-term psychosis. Some rare cases of prolonged negative mental reactions lasting months or even years after taking LSD have been recorded. The DEA sums up potential long-term psychological dangers this way:

> The consequences of LSD use can be deleterious, not merely benign as is commonly perceived. Powerful hallucinations can lead to acute panic reactions when the mental effects cannot be controlled and when the user wishes to end the drug-induced state. While these panic reactions more often than not are resolved successfully over time, prolonged anxiety and psychotic reactions have been reported. The mental effects can cause psychotic crises and compound existing psychiatric problems.[23]

LSD has been called a psychomimetic drug because it can produce a state of mind similar to classic psychoses, such as schizophrenia, found in people who are mentally ill. According to the American Academy of Child and Adolescent Psychiatry, a psychosis is "characterized by extreme impairment of a person's ability to think clearly, respond emotionally, communicate effectively, understand reality, and behave appropriately."[24] In a 1970 paper,

Drs. George S. Glass and Malcolm B. Bowers of the Connecticut Mental Health Center in New Haven reported on four cases of psychosis in young male LSD users that required prolonged hospitalization. According to the doctors, the patients' personalities were believed to have changed drastically after heavy LSD use.

Heavy LSD use can dramatically alter personality, leading to acute anxiety and depression.

They noted that the young men were withdrawn and that their thought processes were bizarre and compounded by paranoid delusions.

In some cases, LSD has been blamed for delayed psychoses, in which people with no prior history of psychosis or any other psychiatric problems experience their first psychotic symptoms weeks, months, or years after taking LSD. In one such case reported in the *New England Journal of Medicine* in 1965, a young man went to the admitting office of a hospital in a state of panic. He was having distorted visions and experiencing feelings and fears that were similar to ones he had had while taking LSD a few months earlier. The doctors reported that these symptoms went away but occurred again during situations that caused the young man to feel fear or anxiety.

LSD researchers have cautioned against relating psychosis with prior LSD use. They point out that many factors can contribute to psychosis, such as the use of other drugs, pre-existing psychiatric illness, and a history of psychiatric illness in the family. Nev-

In rare instances, LSD has been blamed for cases of delayed psychosis. Such conditions require hospitalization for treatment.

ertheless, there may be a relationship between LSD and long-term psychosis. As noted by the Canadian Government Commission:

> Many investigators contend that such extreme experiences occur only in individuals already predisposed to psychotic reaction, and are simply precipitated by the stress of a "bad trip." On the other hand, numerous examples have occurred in persons without obvious prior pathology, and it would appear that there is no satisfactory method for predicting who might suffer a serious adverse reaction.[25]

LSD Flashbacks

In contrast to long-term psychosis, flashbacks, another side effect associated with LSD, occur more commonly and have been well documented since the 1960s. According to some studies, flashbacks occur in up to 33 percent of healthy people who have used LSD and up to 50 percent of those who have psychiatric problems or illnesses and have used LSD. Flashbacks are a recurrence of the experiences a person has had under the influence of LSD. They occur long after the drug was taken and its immediate effects have worn off. Flashbacks typically involve episodes of visual distortion that can last anywhere from a few seconds to several hours in extreme cases. The person may also have physical symptoms such as tingling and numbness of the skin. Many people who have had flashbacks also report feelings of anxiety, depression, or panic. According to Leigh A. Henderson, "Flashbacks may resemble such altered states of consciousness as hypnosis, daydreaming, and sleepwalking."[26]

Most flashbacks are short term and less intense than the original trip. In addition, the more time that passes after a person has taken the LSD, the less intense and less frequent flashbacks become. Because most flashbacks occur spontaneously and with little warning, they can be dangerous. For example, if a person is driving a car or operating machinery and a flashback occurs, he may injure himself or others. Research has shown that several factors can play a role in bringing on a flashback. Among the most common causes of LSD flashbacks are emotional stress, fatigue, use of other drugs such as marijuana, and dark environments.

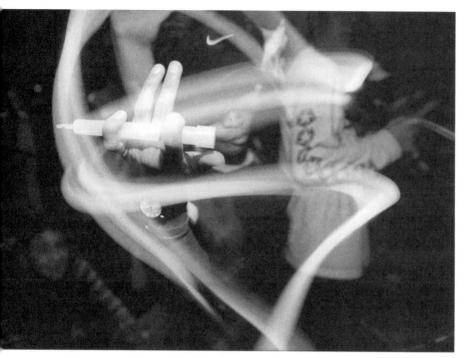

A trail of light from a glow stick is photographed with high-speed film. Flashbacks involving such light trails are a common side effect of LSD.

What Is HPPD?

Although flashbacks seldom occur more than a few months after LSD has been taken, long-term or chronic flashbacks have been documented. The psychiatric community has designated these occurrences as a psychiatric disease called hallucinogen persisting perception disorder (HPPD). Some instances of HPPD have been reported to last five years or more. Most people with HPPD realize that their perceptions do not represent external reality and are due to the aftereffects of LSD. The majority of people with HPPD seek psychiatric help.

For the most part, drug treatment for flashbacks and HPPD have been relatively unsuccessful. Some patients have responded well to antianxiety drugs called benzodiazepines. These drugs can help reduce the intensity and frequency of flashbacks.

Does LSD Use Permanently Change Personality?

With all the various effects that LSD has on a person mentally, another concern is the possibility that chronic LSD use permanently changes personality. An individual's personality is a combination of a variety of mental attributes, including thought processes, behavior, temperament, emotions, and likes and dislikes.

Some LSD users have reported long-term positive changes in their personalities following LSD use, including feeling less anxious and less aggressive. On the other hand, some have reported feeling that their use of LSD has made them feel more anxious and paranoid in their day-to-day lives.

A 1971 study of people who used LSD recreationally found that many seemed to have undergone personality changes. The group as a whole said that after they began to use LSD they were

---

Hofmann's View on LSD and the Mystical Experience

LSD's discoverer, Dr. Albert Hofmann, was first and foremost a scientist. But he did believe, largely based on several experiences he had as a youth, in people's ability to experience higher consciousness or to have a mystical experience. In his book *LSD: My Problem Child*, Hofmann described such experiences he had as a child and concluded, "It was these experiences that shaped the main outlines of my world view and convinced me of the existence of a miraculous, powerful, unfathomable reality that was hidden from everyday sight."

In the foreword to his book, Hofmann acknowledged that LSD and other hallucinogens can cause a "fundamental alteration in our perception of reality" that was similar to a mystical experience and, as such, deserved scientific attention. He also urged the researchers and therapists who were using LSD at the time to exercise extreme caution. He went on to note,

> Deliberate provocation of mystical experience, particularly by LSD and related hallucinogens, in contrast to spontaneous visionary experiences, entails dangers that must not be underestimated. . . . The history of LSD to date amply demonstrates the catastrophic consequences that can ensue when its profound effect is misjudged and the substance is mistaken for a pleasure drug. . . . Wrong and inappropriate use has caused LSD to become my problem child.

Dr. Albert Hofmann, the Swiss chemist who discovered LSD in 1940, believed the drug possessed tremendous therapeutic value.

more likely to be spontaneous and seek excitement and new sensations. On the other hand, they also viewed themselves as somewhat alienated from society. But differentiating between cause and effect is difficult. It is possible that these people used LSD *because* they were spontaneous thrill seekers. Leigh A. Henderson points out, "The existence of such differences in the nonmedical LSD users does not mean that LSD use caused these differences; rather, the two results suggest that LSD attracts a particular type of person."[27] In the end, most researchers agree they do not have enough data to establish a direct link between LSD use and permanent changes in personality.

Despite the potential dangers of LSD use, the drug's effects on the mind have attracted many users over the past four decades. While some characteristics of those who use the drug has changed over the years, LSD use largely remains a phenomenon of youth.

Chapter 3

LSD Use: Yesterday and Today

Over the course of its relatively short history beginning in the late 1940s, LSD emerged from the research laboratory to become a street drug abused by millions. Interestingly, LSD became a cultural phenomenon in the 1960s, and an identifiable subculture of LSD users arose. What is significant is that aspects of this subculture quickly entered and influenced the mainstream, affecting many who never even used the drug.

By 1970 an estimated 1 to 2 million Americans had taken LSD despite the illegality of the drug. Since the 1970s, the use of LSD has dropped dramatically. Although the drug made a strong comeback in the 1990s, LSD use once again appeared to be on the decline during the early years of the twenty-first century.

How Did LSD Become Popular?

By 1963 pirated LSD was being sold as a recreational drug, and within a few short years LSD use exploded. According to the *Consumers Union Report on Licit and Illicit Drugs*, published in 1972, the general public's knowledge of LSD largely came from the publicity the drug received in the media. For the most part, the reports focused on the dangers of LSD. Because some reports

43

indicated that LSD use was rampant among youth, many people came to believe that LSD was a major threat to the very fabric of society. For example, according to the chairman of the 1966 New Jersey Narcotic Drug Study Commission, LSD was "the greatest threat facing the country today . . . more dangerous than the Vietnam war."[28]

On the other side were the proponents of LSD use. Some proponents were health professionals, primarily in the field of psychiatry and psychology, who had experimented with the drug in government-approved research projects. Others experimented with the drug on an unapproved, personal basis on themselves and with friends. These proponents claimed that LSD offered people new insights into themselves and the world around them. Often they made a convincing argument for the use of LSD. As noted in the *Consumers Union Report on Licit and Illicit Drugs:* "The combination of warnings and praise triggered a publicity barrage that grew far out of rational proportion. The net effect was to make LSD familiar to everyone in the land, and to arouse nationwide curiosity. From curiosity to experimentation is only one short step."[29]

Leary and LSD

LSD differed from other illegal drugs in the 1960s in that it attracted highly educated and articulate people, many of whom taught or attended classes at some of the most prestigious colleges in the United States. Some of them, such as psychologist and Harvard professor Timothy Leary and noted author Ken Kesey, openly proposed that LSD could benefit the general populace.

Leary, more than anyone else, is recognized as the person who firmly placed LSD in the public's consciousness in the 1960s. While conducting research at the Department of Social Relations and the Graduate School of Education at Harvard University, Leary and his colleague Richard Alpert began experimenting with the drug on themselves. The duo soon began to widen their circle of experimentation and gave the drug to other colleagues, stu-

Psychologist and Harvard University professor Timothy Leary believed LSD to be a key to higher consciousness.

dents, and artists, including noted poet Allen Ginsberg and writer Jack Kerouac.

Eventually, Leary and Alpert became the subject of an investigation by the Food and Drug Administration and Massachusetts law enforcement officials. While Harvard authorities warned students against taking LSD, Leary and Alpert continued to recommend its use, claiming that it led to a higher level of consciousness. A *Life* magazine exposé on LSD use reported, "Leary and Alpert consider LSD 'a sacred biochemical' that clears the path to mystic understanding."[30]

Leary's Ultimate Trip

Although he is best known as the pied piper of the acid generation, Timothy Leary also had a PhD in psychology and was the author of twenty-seven books and monographs and approximately 250 articles. Born in 1920, Leary became a psychology professor and taught both at the University of California, Berkeley, and Harvard University. He was introduced to hallucinogens while conducting research on Latin American healing techniques in the 1950s. In 1960 he took the hallucinogenic psilocybin mushrooms while on vacation in Mexico. When he took LSD for the first time in 1962, he later recalled that it was the most shattering experience of his life.

Leary and Alpert were dismissed from Harvard in 1963 for promoting LSD use, but Leary continued to speak out about the benefits of LSD, quickly becoming a national figure. He formed the League of Spiritual Discovery, which was an LSD advocacy group. Leary is also credited with coining the catchphrase "Turn on, tune in, and drop out," meaning that people could liberate their minds through the use of LSD and other mind-altering drugs.

Birth of the LSD Subculture

Although LSD was banned by the U.S. federal government in 1967, the drug had already captured the nation's attention. While reports about LSD's intense psychological effects were frightening, they also attracted a growing interest in the drug. The primary interest was among the nation's youth, many of whom appeared to be following Leary's edict to "turn on" to LSD and "drop out" of society. The use of LSD also became more acceptable because of the rise in overall illegal drug use—especially marijuana—among America's middle-class youth.

Many young people saw the use of LSD as a type of rebellion and rejection of middle-class values that emphasize acquiring material things and financial success. Increasingly displeased with society, they became active in civil rights, protests against the Vietnam War, and other efforts at social change. Admittedly, some youths took the drug only because of the intense high it provided.

But most believed that LSD offered a portal through which they could gain a new perspective on society and life itself. Noted educator and author Linda Bayer summed up the 1960s counterculture movement, that is, a movement espousing lifestyles and values opposed to those of the norm, this way: "Protest music, antiwar sentiments, long hair, permissive sexual behavior, a rejection of U.S. materialism, and the use of mind altering drugs all combined to set young people apart from the society of their elders."[31]

As the talk about LSD spread throughout college campuses, a distinct counterculture began to emerge. By 1965 the counterculture movement was prominent and even reported on by the media.

Two teenagers dance at an LSD party hosted by author Ken Kesey. Throughout the 1960s, many middle-class teenagers experimented with LSD as a form of rebellion.

As noted by psychiatrist Lester Grinspoon and *Harvard Mental Health Letter* associate editor James B. Bakalar, the counterculture movement was largely made up of children of affluence and leisure who did not feel as though they were a part of mainstream society. For some college-educated whites, wrote the authors, the largely conservative cultural institutions of religion and government were meaningless in a society undergoing severe turmoil, including the unpopular war in Vietnam and the assassinations of government and civic leaders like President John F. Kennedy and Martin Luther King Jr. The authors state, "[These youth] needed new symbols and rituals to shape beliefs and guide action."[32]

LSD Influences Mainstream Culture

While the vast majority of people in the United States did not use LSD, in the late 1960s and early 1970s the LSD-influenced counterculture movement affected many aspects of mainstream society and culture, from music and art to questions about life itself. Perhaps most surprisingly, mainstream society began to question some traditional American values as well.

A prime example of the LSD counterculture's influence on American values concerned the public's views of God and religion. The vast majority of Americans have traditionally followed Western faiths, such as Christianity or Judaism, which generally stress looking outward to a God that is separate from and beyond the world. In contrast, Eastern religions, such as Buddhism, focus on looking for God within. These religions stress the need for practicing meditation and other techniques as a way to achieve mystical experiences and a better understanding of life. Many LSD users were claiming that taking LSD provided similar experiences, and their reports helped bring these uncommon attitudes to the general public's attention. As a result, Eastern religions became more popular with many Americans who were searching for alternative answers to questions about life. Lester Grinspoon and James B. Bakalar point out, "LSD made a mass phenomenon of attitudes and ideas that had been the property of solitary mystics, esoteric religions, eccentric cults, or literary cliques."[33]

Many hippies, like these at a 1967 San Francisco love-in, promoted the use of mind-altering drugs as one way to reject the values of mainstream society.

Most important was the LSD subculture's influence on people who never used drugs. As Grinspoon and Bakalar state: "Many people experienced a kind of cultural contact high without taking drugs at all."[34] Part of this was reflected in new art, music, and recreation that mirrored changing attitudes about life. Bright, swirling colors characterized art and fashion and came to be known as "psychedelic." Youths not necessarily involved in LSD began to attend dances and other events featuring elaborate light shows and pulsating sounds that were meant to imitate the sensory effects of LSD, as well as to heighten these effects for those who were taking the drug. These types of light shows continued well into the late 1970s at discos and have experienced a resurgence at modern parties.

LSD and the Arts

In addition to the nation's youth, many artists and musicians were also experimenting with LSD. Rock music was so heavily influenced by the LSD experience that several bands created a musical style called "acid rock." Acid rock typically featured loud music, long instrumental improvisations, or jamming, and technical innovations such as fuzz tone, feedback, and synthesizers. To further mimic some of the effects associated with LSD, many live musical performances also included light shows.

The most notable acid rock band was the San Francisco–based group called the Warlocks, who later changed their name to The Grateful Dead. Soon much of the rock-and-roll of the late 1960s

The acid rock band The Grateful Dead incorporated lengthy jamming sessions and light shows in their concerts to enhance the effects of LSD.

referred to LSD, including songs such as "Eight Miles High," by the Byrds, and "White Rabbit," by Jefferson Airplane. It was also generally thought that the Beatles' song "Lucy in the Sky with Diamonds" stood for LSD, and as proof many pointed to the song's surrealistic lyrics.

Books and literature about or influenced by LSD appeared on bookshelves around the country. As early as 1962, Alan Watts attempted to describe his experiences while taking LSD and other hallucinogens in his book *The Joyous Cosmology*. The book included an introduction by Timothy Leary and Richard Alpert, who noted, "Alan Watts spells out in eloquent detail his drug-induced visionary moments. He is, of course, attempting the impossible—to describe in words (which always lie) that which is beyond words."[35] This book and others like it were notable because people who had never used LSD enjoyed reading them.

The *New York Times* best-seller *One Flew Over the Cuckoo's Nest* was also published in 1962. The book was partially based on author Ken Kesey's LSD experiments. The book was an early counterculture statement, as it told a story that presented mainstream society as something that sought to make everyone conform while stamping out individual freedom.

Six years later, in 1968, author Tom Wolfe's *Electric Kool-Aid Acid Test* also became a *New York Times* best-seller. In the book, Wolfe recounts the efforts of Kesey and his group of "Merry Pranksters" as they travel the country in a psychedelic-painted bus taking LSD and conducting "acid tests." LSD was liberally distributed to those who attended these tests, which were essentially big parties sometimes attended by hundreds of people, a few of whom did not know they were taking the drug.

According to Wolfe, Kesey's acid tests of the mid-1960s were the biggest influence on introducing the LSD subculture to the mainstream. Kesey and his friends traveled throughout California and other parts of the country conducting their tests and attracting a growing number of young people, who began to spread the word. As a result, Kesey and his friends' outrageous clothing style, incorporating swirling colors and Day-Glo paints, was becoming popular on college campuses around the country. As predicted by Wolfe in the *Electric Kool-Aid Acid Test*, the counterculture and the art it influenced became commonplace in the form of psychedelic T-shirts, posters, and other art.

The End of an Era

Even though psychedelic art and music remained popular, the LSD subculture began to dissipate by the beginning of the 1970s as the use of LSD began a dramatic decline. By then even Kesey had denounced the effects of LSD as delusional and its curative properties as only temporary.

Furthermore, the counterculture movement's dedication to peace and love had undergone a serious examination. For example, in 1969 Charles Manson and his family of followers went on a murder spree, killing actress Sharon Tate and several others. It was soon publicized that Manson and his followers took LSD regularly and that Manson had used LSD and other drugs to help control the minds of his followers.

Further reducing the use of LSD was the widespread media attention on the drug's various dangers. As it became widely known that the drug's effects could be unpleasant and that LSD could potentially damage the body and mind, LSD use declined.

A New Era of LSD Use

Although by the 1980s LSD use had greatly declined, it made a resurgence in the 1990s, primarily among teenagers. A survey conducted by Monitoring the Future Study found that 13.6 percent of 1997's high school seniors had experimented with LSD at least once compared to only 7.2 percent in 1986.

Many sociologists and drug experts blamed LSD's resurgence on a lack of knowledge about the drug among the nation's young people. Part of this stemmed from the fact that drug education efforts were focusing on other drugs, because LSD did not appear to be the problem it once had been. As a result, between 1991 and 1996, the percentage of high school seniors who said they disapproved of LSD use even once or twice fell from 90 to 80 per-

Ken Kesey traveled the country in a psychedelic-painted bus and hosted parties known as acid tests, at which LSD was freely distributed.

cent. In a 1997 report published by the U.S. Department of Justice's National Institute of Justice, author Dana Hunt noted that renewed interest in hallucinogens may be due to more teenagers perceiving LSD as a safe drug. The high school survey data indicate a significant decline in the percentage of seniors who feel that trying LSD or using it regularly is a great risk.

Factors in LSD Resurgence of the 1990s

In addition to a lack of knowledge about LSD's potentially harmful effects, experts believed that several factors led to the drug's resurgence. Unlike most drugs, LSD is relatively inexpensive. It is also produced in laboratories within the United States, so people who distribute and sell the drug do not have to smuggle it into the country. Because LSD is cheap and easily attained, more people began to use it.

The rise in hallucinogen use in the 1990s also was associated with the growth of "raves," underground dance parties held in large halls, warehouses, or deserted areas that begin late at night and generally continue until dawn. Advertised as all-ages parties and rarely serving alcohol, raves cater to people under the age of

Raves and LSD

As a result of LSD and other rampant illegal drug use at dance parties known as raves, many cities such as Chicago, Denver, and New York have begun anti-rave initiatives. The federal Drug Enforcement Administration has also begun a national educational campaign warning about raves and drugs such as LSD.

In 2002 Senator Joseph Biden introduced a law that eventually passed in 2003 as the Illicit Drug Anti-Proliferation Act. The act notes: "Each year tens of thousands of young people are initiated into the drug culture at 'rave' parties or events (all-night, alcohol-free dance parties typically featuring loud, pounding dance music)." Designed to enable law enforcement to arrest rave and other event organizers, the bill states its goal this way: "To prohibit an individual from knowingly opening, maintaining, managing, controlling, renting, leasing, making available for use, or profiting from any place for the purpose of manufacturing, distributing, or using any controlled substance, and for other purposes."

Congress has also introduced new bills that would make it even easier to hold event sponsors liable for drug use by those in attendance. These bills explicitly target raves.

twenty-one. According to the National Drug Intelligence Center, criminals recognized a profit could be made by targeting teens and began to promote drug usage at raves. As a result, a variety of hallucinogens became popular, including LSD. Many ravers mistakenly came to believe that LSD could not be harmful if it was used "responsibly." Although no concrete statistics are available, hundreds of teenagers and young adults have overdosed on drugs at raves and some of them have died, although none of the deaths have been linked directly to LSD.

One person who had a negative reaction to LSD at a rave described the experience this way:

> I tried to control the drug in my body but I couldn't, it was just too strong for me. I couldn't relax either my body or my mind, it was busy taking over. So many thoughts and emotions flooded my being and I became terrified and scared not knowing what was going on! The more I tried to relax the more anxious I became. I went to the dance floor and started dancing, hoping it would stop and go away. But the music and the people scared me.[36]

Much like the psychedelic concerts and parties of the 1960s, raves incorporate music and light shows designed to enhance or mimic the effects of hallucinogenic drugs. Rave music, often featuring repetitive computer-generated sounds, has branched out into several categories, including techno, trance, progressive trance, cybertrance, tech step, and big beat. Just like acid rock decades earlier, this music has also reached the mainstream. Rave toys and jewelry, such as colorful bracelets and necklaces with pacifiers, usually feature bright, flashing lights that enhance the hallucinogenic effects of LSD and other drugs.

LSD Users of the 1990s

The LSD users of the 1990s are much younger than those of the 1960s. In addition, many more of those who use LSD have experimented with it even before they have reached high school. According to the National Household Survey on Drug Abuse, by 1993 13.2 million Americans twelve years of age or older reported that they had used LSD at least once compared to 8.1 million in 1985.

Dana Hunt has noted that today's LSD users are similar to users in the 1960s in that they are primarily middle-class white youths. In fact, throughout its history of illegal use, LSD has been used mainly by whites. According to a 1994 Monitoring the Future Study, 8 percent of white high school seniors reported using LSD in the prior twelve months, compared with less than 1 percent of African American and 5 percent of Hispanic seniors.

Just as in the past, many modern users report taking LSD to set them apart from their parents and elders and to escape their responsibilities. Researchers James MacDonald and Michael Agar, who interviewed several young LSD users, noted: "Adults represented a set of rules centered on stability, order, and predictability that made no sense at all during a trip. The adult world represented the problem that a trip was designed to solve."[37]

LSD Use Declines Once Again

Since 1996 the percentage of teenagers who use LSD has dropped. In 2001, University of Michigan and Monitoring the

Future researcher Lloyd D. Johnston stated: "We have seen a considerable decline of LSD use over the past five years."[38]

The decline in LSD use in the early part of the twenty-first century coincided with a decline in overall drug use among 12-year-olds and teenagers. A 2003 Monitoring the Future survey revealed an 11 percent decline in drug use by eighth-, tenth-, and twelfth-grade students over the previous two years. According to a 2003 press release from the U.S. Department of Health and Human Services, the number of youths who had used LSD fell 43 percent between 2001 and 2003.

Debate over Why LSD Use Declined

The reasons behind the steady reduction in LSD use have been debated. In 2001 social scientists and researcher Lloyd D. Johnston noted that the decline was "not because youngsters are coming to see the drug as more dangerous." Instead, according to Johnston, just the opposite was occurring, as fewer students were likely to perceive the risks and disapproval associated with LSD use. Johnston went on to note, "We think the reduction in LSD

A teenager dances at a rave, where computer-generated music and light shows are used to enhance the effects of LSD and other hallucinogenic drugs.

Slang Terms for LSD

Just like many other illegal street drugs, LSD has many nicknames or slang terms, one of the most common being "acid." Some of the nicknames indicate the forms in which LSD is sold. For example, LSD available in sugar cubes is often referred to simply as "cubes" and "windowpane" refers to LSD in a gelatin form. The paper form of LSD is usually referred to as "blotter acid" or "tabs." Some of the paper forms are also referred to by the illustrations or designs on them, such as "Bart Simpsons," "Russian sickles," and "strawberries." Among the other most common nicknames for LSD are "orange sunshine," "stamps," "microdots," "orange barrels," "domes," "California sunshine," "Owsley," "sugar," and "Sandoz."

use may be occurring because ecstasy is displacing it as a drug of choice [and] fewer students have friends who are [LSD] users."[39]

By 2003, with LSD use at its lowest level in the nearly three-decade history of the Monitoring the Future Study, government officials were touting government and educational efforts as the reason for reduced LSD use. John Walters, director of the federal Office of National Drug Control Policy, noted, "Fewer teens are using drugs because of the deliberate and serious messages they have received about the dangers of drugs from their parents, leaders, and prevention efforts like our National Youth Anti-Drug Media Campaign."[40]

Indeed, data shows that media campaigns targeting young people and outlining the dangers of LSD and other drugs appear to be having a positive impact. Others continue to disagree about the effectiveness of the educational campaigns. According to Marsha Rosenbaum, director of the Safety First project with the Drug Policy Alliance, a decline in drug use by teens over a short period of time is inconsequential because drug use is cyclical "and has gone up and down and then up and down again in the 25-year history of the Monitoring the Future survey."[41]

According to the view of Rosenbaum and others, the recreational use of LSD likely will increase again in the future. In the meantime the federal government and law enforcement agencies have continued to wage an ongoing battle against LSD use.

Chapter 4

LSD and the Law

LSD was once a legal drug studied for use in psychiatric patients, but its increasing abuse by a growing population of young people resulted in widespread concern and legislation outlawing LSD. As a result, making, selling, and using LSD have been illegal in the United States and most other industrialized countries for nearly four decades.

The U.S. Food and Drug Administration and the Drug Enforcement Administration have taken a strong stance on LSD manufacturing and use, including its use in therapy and for scientific research. Over the years, the battle against illegal LSD use has faced many obstacles. At the same time, the overall supply of LSD has remained relatively constant for nearly twenty-five years.

Another major problem began to emerge in the early 1960s. In 1963 Sandoz, the drug company that produced pharmaceutical LSD, let its patent rights for producing LSD expire. As a result, it no longer controlled LSD's legal production, which Sandoz had limited for use by the medical community. This change meant that anyone could legally manufacture and distribute the drug since neither the United States nor any other country had laws to control LSD. Soon various people began to manufacture LSD, and the drug began to be sold on the street.

LSD Is Made Illegal

The United States and other governments began to consider outlawing LSD as public concern grew over the increasing number of people who were taking the drug recreationally and without the supervision of a doctor. Concerns were magnified when hospitals began reporting that their staffs were treating more and more panic attack episodes and other side effects in young people who had taken the drug. Even Albert Hofmann, LSD's discoverer, was upset by its illegal use. Hofmann recalled, "Since my self-experiment had revealed LSD in its terrifying, demonic aspect, the last thing I could have expected was that this substance could ever find application as anything approaching a pleasure drug."[42]

Timothy Leary is arrested on a narcotics charge in 1966. That year, Congress outlawed the manufacturing and sale of LSD and other hallucinogenics.

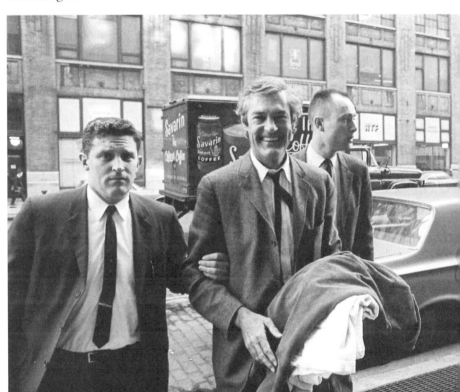

As noted in a *Life* article, "At any rate, the genie of LSD, with all its tantalizing possibilities for good and evil, is out in the open."[43] It did not take long for the government to try to put the genie back in the bottle. In 1966 Congress passed the Drug Abuse Control Amendment, which banned the individual manufacturing or sale of LSD and other similar hallucinogens. The law greatly restricted LSD by allowing only legitimate wholesale manufacturing, distribution, and use in research and medical situations. While illegal manufacturing and sale could be prosecuted, the law did not address personal possession of the drug. Personal use of LSD was still not punishable under the law as long as the individual was not making or selling the drug.

Social Views Impact Medical Research

The growing public outcry and government concerns over LSD use soon began to affect medical research of the drug. Before long, the FDA began to demand that LSD researchers halt their studies and return all their supplies of LSD. Some said the FDA was concerned for patient safety and was responding to those in the medical profession who believed the drug was potentially dangerous. Others believed that the use of LSD in therapy and research had to be banned to prevent people from thinking the drug was safe. In 1965 the FDA shut down numerous LSD research projects. The following year, Sandoz Pharmaceuticals halted LSD's distribution to the United States.

In 1966 congressional hearings were held to discuss the government's ban on LSD research. Some politicians argued that research with the drug should continue. Senator Robert Kennedy, for example, wondered how a drug that was considered so valuable six months earlier had suddenly become so despised. "Perhaps," Kennedy said, "we have lost sight of the fact that [LSD] can be very, very helpful in our society if used properly."[44]

Many researchers also spoke out against the government's growing restrictions on LSD research. Speaking before a meeting of the American Psychiatric Association, LSD researcher Dr. Stephen Szara commented, "It is my belief that it would be most

Senator Robert Kennedy argued that medical research with LSD should continue despite the illegality of the drug.

unfortunate if we were to permit undue hysteria to destroy a valuable tool of science, and evaporate an eventual hope for the many hopeless."[45]

Despite protests from some in the scientific community, the FDA and NIMH remained skeptical of LSD research and established the Psychotomimetic Advisory Committe in 1967 to review current research with the drug. Shortly afterward, the NIMH essentially halted all but a few of its own sponsored research projects involving LSD. This reduction in research stemmed from several factors, including concern for patient safety, a lack of strong scientific evidence that the drug was beneficial in any way, and increasing pressure from the government and the general public who saw the drug as dangerous.

The Controlled Substances Act

In 1970 the U.S. Congress passed the Controlled Substances Act. According to the DEA, this act serves as the legal foundation of the government's fight against the abuse of drugs and other substances. When the Controlled Substances Act was passed, it consolidated numerous laws regulating the manufacture and distribution of a variety of drugs, including LSD. It put all federally regulated substances into one of five schedules. This placement is based upon the substance's medicinal value, harmfulness, and potential for abuse or addiction.

Under the law, LSD was and continues to be placed in Schedule 1, which is reserved for what are believed to be the most dangerous drugs. LSD and all other Schedule 1 drugs have been defined as drugs that have a high potential for abuse. They are not accepted for medical use in the United States because

Police officers search for drugs among items seized from a car. The law considers LSD to be a very dangerous drug, and possession of it is a serious crime.

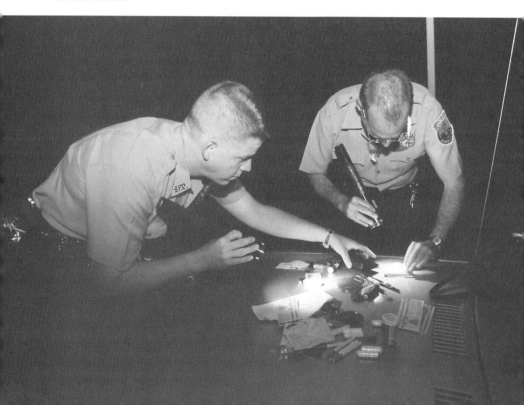

they are believed to be potentially unsafe even under medical supervision. This classification restricted LSD research to non-human subjects unless a special approval was granted by the FDA.

While the United States took the lead in banning LSD, other countries soon followed. In 1971 the United Nations' Convention on Psychotropic Substances required all participating parties or nations to prohibit LSD, making it illegal in most of Europe. In 1974, the NIMH halted all research with the drug when a NIMH research task force declared that there were no medical benefits associated with LSD.

Obstacles in Stopping LSD Use

Although sanctioned supplies of LSD were difficult to obtain, the illegal manufacture and sale of the drug continued at a fast pace. For more than thirty years the DEA, formerly the Bureau of Narcotics and Dangerous Drugs, has battled the illegal manufacture, sale, and use of LSD. Despite the DEA's efforts, the drug has continued to be used by high school and college students in virtually every state.

The DEA has noted that several factors play a role in the continued availability of LSD. Although large amounts of LSD have been seized by law enforcement over the years and numerous distributors have been arrested and imprisoned, most of those at the higher levels of illegal manufacturing have continued to evade capture. This is in part because discovering LSD manufacturing labs is so difficult. The labs are often makeshift and can be set up almost anywhere, from people's basements to old farm buildings. The labs do not stay in continuous production and are easily moved to different sites. As the DEA points out, "Few LSD laboratories have ever been seized in the United States because of infrequent and irregular production cycles."[46]

Capturing LSD dealers is also difficult. In a 1995 report, "LSD in the United States," the DEA noted that there were probably fewer than a dozen people responsible for manufacturing all of the LSD in the United States. Many of these people are thought to have been in the LSD business since the 1960s and are experienced in eluding law enforcement. The DEA further noted, "Drug Law enforcement officials have surmised that LSD chemists and top echelon traffickers form an insider's fraternity of sorts. They successfully have remained at large because there are so few of them."[47]

In addition to the relatively few and close-knit suppliers of LSD who manufacture the drug in large quantitites, the DEA must consider that the drug's distribution is different from that of most other drugs. Since LSD is lightweight and odorless, it is distributed in large quantities through mail-order sales via the U.S. Postal Service, Federal Express, and other mailing services. In this marketplace, the sellers are virtually unknown to the buyers, keeping the upper-level traffickers hidden from law enforcement investigations. The drug is also distributed through networks that have been established for many years and are difficult for undercover DEA agents to infiltrate.

Areas of Illegal Distribution and Sale
The DEA says that LSD production can be pinpointed to several areas in the United States. Over most of the four decades of illegal LSD use, the drug has been produced primarily in San Francisco, northern California, and the Pacific Northwest. The DEA believes that the San Francisco manufacturer ships liquid LSD throughout the United States. Once it reaches its destination, the LSD is applied to paper and sold on an individual basis. More recently, LSD production has also been found in the Midwest. In 2000 the DEA seized an LSD laboratory that was located in an old missile silo in Kansas. Over ninety pounds of the drug were confiscated.

For many years the DEA has also traced the sale of large quantities of LSD to distributors located at acid rock concerts, particularly those of the Grateful Dead. According to the DEA, the concerts are places where both large-scale and individual sales occur. Likewise, dealers have been targeted and arrested by undercover agents at raves.

DEA Agents Find Their Men

Although the U.S. Drug Enforcement Administration has long admitted to difficulty in making major LSD busts, the agency made its largest LSD lab seizure in 2000. DEA agents seized 90.86 pounds of LSD and a complete LSD lab in the bust. (In its entire history, the DEA has made only four seizures of complete LSD labs.) According to the DEA, the lab was discovered packed away in an abandoned missile silo in Wamego, Kansas. Two people were later arrested as they tried to move the illegal lab.

The DEA noted that the two men produced about 2.2 pounds of LSD every five weeks at a cost of less than one cent per dose. The single doses would then sell for as much as $10. During the men's trial, the DEA charged that they were among the highest-level LSD producers and traffickers in the country. The men were eventually found guilty of LSD production and trafficking. One of them received life imprisonment without parole and the other thirty years' imprisonment without parole. In a November 25, 2003, DEA news release, Special Agent in Charge William J. Renton Jr. noted:

> These defendants were proven, by overwhelming evidence, to be responsible for the illicit manufacture of the majority of the LSD sold in this nation. The proof of the significance of these prosecutions and convictions lies in the fact that LSD availability in the United States was reduced by 95% in the two years following their arrest.

LSD Penalties

Since LSD is illegal throughout the United States, anyone caught with any amount of LSD could possibly spend time in jail. State laws vary for simple possession and use of LSD. Simple possession means that the person possesses enough of a drug for personal use only and not for sale. In New Jersey and Utah, for example, simple possession of LSD could lead to a prison term of up to five years. In Utah the penalty could also include a fine of up to $5,000, and in New Jersey the fine could be up to $25,000. Other states may have much harsher penalties. In Louisiana, for example, someone arrested for possession of LSD could receive a prison sentence of up to ten years of hard labor.

For the most part, however, law enforcement officials are interested in punishing the people who manufacture and sell LSD. Under federal law in the United States, trafficking of LSD

Two tabs on a finger illustrate the very small size of an LSD dose. The drug is also odorless, making detection difficult for drug agents.

is defined as possession of a minimum of one gram of LSD. Considering that LSD is extremely lightweight, one gram represents a considerable amount of the drug, about ten thousand doses. For a first offense involving the possession of one to nine grams of LSD, the penalty is five to forty years in prison and a fine of up to $5 million. A second offense has a minimum prison sentence of ten years to life and a fine of $10 million. These penalties essentially double for possession and trafficking of ten grams or more of LSD.

LSD and Mandatory Sentencing

Mandatory minimum sentences play an integral role in the sentencing of people convicted for LSD possession and trafficking. Mandatory minimum sentences standardize the amount of time a person must spend in prison for committing certain crimes. They were established by Congress in 1986 as a way to deter certain crimes by establishing harsher universal penalties. In the case of LSD and other drugs, sentencing is based on the amount of the drug involved.

Many in the federal government and law enforcement support mandatory minimum sentences for LSD and other drugs. Federal prosecutors contend that the harsh sentences are necessary because they provide law enforcement with a tool for breaking drug syndicates. For example, if people caught dealing LSD or other drugs know that they face a minimum sentence of at least five years, law enforcement can cut a deal with them to reduce their sentences. They might receive a reduced sentence by naming the people who are higher up in the drug-dealing organization.

The possession and sale of LSD are crimes subject to mandatory minimum sentences in many states.

Those who favor mandatory minimums see them as a fair punishment for people who break the law. In an interview on the Public Broadcasting Service show *Frontline*, former narcotics agent Bill Alden discussed mandatory minimums: "People violated the law with premeditation. It's not a crime of passion. You think about what you're going to do. You really need to think—I have to think about the consequences of my actions daily. I know that I'm accountable for what I do, and I have to calculate what I do based on that."[48]

Mandatory minimum supporters also are convinced that such laws help drive drug dealers from the streets and discourage people from getting into the business. Supporters observe that since mandatory minimums were put into effect, there has been a significant decrease in crime throughout the United States. Candace McCoy, a criminal justice professor at Rutgers University, has noted that the laws have succeeded: "They proved that politicians and the public could be rough and tough, and meant to be serious about stopping drugs."[49]

Arguments Against Mandatory Minimums

Many groups and people, including those within the justice system, like U.S. Supreme Court Justice Stephen Breyer, have argued against mandatory minimums. One of the most common arguments is that mandatory minimum sentences give judges little leeway in considering individual circumstances. In the case of LSD, sentencing is based solely on the amount of the drug involved. As a result, a first-time offender could receive the same sentence as a career drug dealer.

Families Against Mandatory Minimums (FAMM), a nonprofit foundation, challenges penalties required by mandatory minimum sentencing laws. The organization notes that most people serving time in prison for drug offenses, including LSD, are low-level dealers selling small amounts of the drugs and not involved in the trafficking of large quantities. According to the U.S. Sentencing Commission, only 11 percent of people in federal prisons on drug charges are high-level drug traffickers.

FAMM has also pointed out that high-level dealers of LSD and other drugs are better able to make a deal to reduce their sentences because they are more likely than low-level dealers to know how the drug organization works and who is in charge. As a result, the low-level dealer, who does not have information that law enforcement wants, is not able to get a reduced sentence. Accord-

Michigan Repeals Mandatory Minimums

Some states are turning away from mandatory minimum sentencing for many crimes, including drug possession. On December 12, 2002, a majority of the Michigan Senate passed a historic package that eliminated most of the state's mandatory minimum sentences for drug offenses. The Michigan move involved the passing of three sentencing reform bills that eliminate the ten-year minimum sentences and allow judges to sentence an offender for any time up to twenty years. The new law also enables drug offenders to become eligible for early parole, depending on a review board. In a news release issued by the Families Against Mandatory Minimums (FAMM), Michigan representative Bill McConico said:

> This major step brings fairness back to the judicial system in Michigan. The overwhelming bipartisan support for this legislation shows it is not a partisan issue. We were able to unite Republicans, Democrats, prosecutors, judges and families in the common cause of sentencing justice. Now we can reunite families, reallocate resources and allow judges to do their job.

In the FAMM news release, David Morse, president of the Prosecuting Attorneys Association of Michigan, stated,

> Michigan's prosecutors recognize that an effective drug policy is a combination of criminal justice strategies, readily available drug treatment programs, incarceration where appropriate, and prevention activities in schools, businesses, and homes. That is why we support a responsible approach to replacing the mandatory minimum sentences for drug crimes with sentences that are appropriate for the crime.

ing to FAMM, "Low-level defendants frequently serve longer sentences than those at the top of the drug trade."[50]

Some point to one case highlighted by Court TV as a prime example of the unfairness of mandatory minimums. A twenty-year-old college woman with no criminal record was sentenced to a long prison term after buying her boyfriend thirty paper sheets of LSD at a Grateful Dead concert. When the boyfriend was arrested, he cut a deal and turned his ex-girlfriend in. She was sentenced to ten years. Although the woman was eventually pardoned by President Bill Clinton prior to his leaving office in 2000, Court TV reporter Harriet Ryan pointed out that the woman was "hardly the type of drug kingpin the public imagined when congress passed popular mandatory minimums."[51]

The War on Drugs

Mandatory minimums for LSD are just one part of the "war on drugs." President Richard M. Nixon first used the term in 1972 to describe the government's various programs and efforts at stopping the sale and use of illegal drugs. President Ronald Reagan in the 1980s created a cabinet position to help direct the war. The person who holds this position is referred to as the "drug czar."

The war on drugs is a complex set of government policies and actions that include law enforcement and legal penalties, campaigns designed to inform the public about the dangers of drugs, and efforts to stop the manufacture of illegal drugs in other countries and their entry into the United States. Proponents of the war

In 1972 former president Richard Nixon (second from left) confers with advisers as he designs the strategy for his war on drugs.

on drugs believe that it can be effective in stopping illegal drug usage and particularly in preventing younger people from trying drugs.

Drug czar John P. Walters has testified before the U.S. House Appropriations Subcommittee on the overall success of the war on drugs, declaring:

> Our efforts to reduce substance abuse in America have been far-reaching and diverse. We are working with the nation's top scientists to make important breakthroughs in the field of addiction research; we are providing cutting-edge technology to the state and local public safety officers who are our first line of defense against drug traffickers; we are supporting community anti-drug coalitions in their grassroots efforts to prevent and reduce drug use in our cities and towns; and we are constantly improving the most comprehensive public health advertising campaign in history. The results of these efforts are paying off: National surveys show that youth drug use is at its lowest levels in nearly a decade.[52]

In 2002, then–drug czar Asa Hutchinson noted that the drug war has been successful in that overall drug use in the United States has been reduced by 50 percent over the last 20 years. Two years later, Walters and Health and Human Services Secretary Tommy G. Thompson pointed to the 2003 Monitoring the Future survey as evidence that the war was having a positive effect. The survey showed that 400,000 fewer teens had used drugs from 2001 to 2003.

As for the effectiveness of the war on drugs in battling LSD use in particular, Walters noted in a message to the U.S. Congress, "Among teens, some drugs—such as LSD—have dropped to record low levels of use."[53] The government attributed much of the reduction to media campaigns outlining the dangers of illegal drug use.

The War Debate

Since the war on drugs began, arrest rates and drug seizures have increased greatly. But over the years, the war on drugs has fostered a strong legal and government debate about its overall success. Many see the war as a failure, noting that it focuses more on law enforcement and apprehension of offenders than on prevention and treatment programs. According to former U.S. Supreme Court Justice Warren Burger, "We must accept that to confine offenders behind walls without trying to change them is an expensive folly with short-term benefits."[54]

Many people point out that arresting and sending drug users to prison is much more expensive than establishing programs to stop people from using drugs in the first place. In 1997 Barry McCaffrey, then the director of the Office of National Drug Control Policy, noted that the government allocates far more funds for law enforcement than for high school prevention programs: "We have more people in prison than any other country in the world. We are willing to spend $22,500 for every prisoner but we aren't willing to spend $2,000 on a high school kid at risk."[55]

Barry McCaffrey, former director of the Office of National Drug Control Policy, was a strong advocate of drug-prevention programs.

In 2001 the Correctional Association of New York, a nonprofit analysis and advocacy organization, issued a report focusing on both New York and federal government drug laws. In their conclusion the authors stated, "The current criminal justice response to nonviolent drug offenders has proven to be ineffective, costly and disproportionately harsh." The report pointed out that nonprison drug treatment programs have been shown to be more effective and cost efficient in battling drug use but that "the prison-only approach remains the nation's primary response to its drug problem."[56]

Even some supporters of the war on drugs feel that it is not enough. For example, former narcotics agent Bill Alden noted

New Campaign Focuses on Prevention

A recent decline in LSD use by young people is one example that the government has pointed to as evidence of the effectiveness of media information campaigns to stop drug abuse. On January 29, 2004, the Office of National Drug Control Policy (ONDCP) announced a new campaign to help stop youth drug use. According to the ONDCP, the initiative takes a new approach to reducing teen substance abuse by focusing on those closest to young drug users, namely their friends, peers, and parents. Called the Early Intervention Initiative, the campaign features television, newspaper, and radio ad campaigns. In an ONDCP news release, director John P. Walters noted:

> We all have the responsibility to stop teen drug use. Parents have a major role to play in helping to stop drug use by their children. But we should not underestimate the power of peers to stop substance abuse among their friends. Early action by both friends and parents can help young people avoid the serious consequences that put their futures at risk.

According to the ONDCP, the Early Intervention Initiative also represents the next step in the agency's strategy of encouraging parental monitoring and involvement to prevent youth drug use. The campaign also features a Web site called Freevibe.com that provides young people with information and news about drug use and how they can help friends who may be abusing drugs.

during his *Frontline* interview that the government needed to have a larger commitment to fighting drugs than its war on drugs campaign. When asked what his experience as a narcotics agent had taught him about controlling illegal drug use, Alden said, "Ultimately, the biggest bang for the buck was in preventing it, and in providing the right information to kids, and working with kids, so that they would make the right decision and see the consequences of their behavior."[57]

While the debate continues about punishment for LSD possession and sale, some in the scientific community are calling for the government to reconsider its laws concerning the study of LSD. They say that in addition to having possible medical benefits, LSD can lead to scientific insights into the human mind.

Chapter 5

LSD in Research

In the late 1940s LSD was introduced as a psychiatric wonder drug that could cure or alleviate numerous problems, including alcoholism, criminal behavior, depression, schizophrenia, and even the pain, anxiety, and fear associated with terminal illness. During the 1950s and early 1960s, scientific research with LSD was accepted as mainstream science, and approximately forty thousand patients received LSD as a part of their psychiatric or psychological therapy. Over this same time period, six international conferences were held and more than one thousand scientific papers and several dozen books were written about the use of LSD in medical psychiatry.

As concerns about the dangers of LSD grew, the United States and other governments became increasingly unwilling to fund research projects involving the drug. By the 1990s, research into LSD and other hallucinogens had dwindled to almost nothing. Now a small group of scientists are once again looking to conduct research into the possible medical benefits of LSD and other hallucinogens. While many of their efforts are based on new discoveries about the mind, these scientists are attempting to build support for their research based on much of the early LSD treatment approaches and research.

Early LSD Treatments

Long before the advent of LSD, patients with severe and persistent mental illness underwent drastic treatments that sometimes harmed them. Schizophrenia was often treated with insulin shock therapy, injections of insulin that cause convulsions. Electroconvulsive therapy, which results in memory loss and other side effects, was widely used to treat depression. In extreme cases, mentally ill patients received a lobotomy, a major surgery in which doctors operated on the frontal lobe of their brain. Overall, the effectiveness of these therapies was questionable and the risks were great.

A team of scientists conducts an experiment in 1955 to determine the usefulness of LSD in psychotherapy.

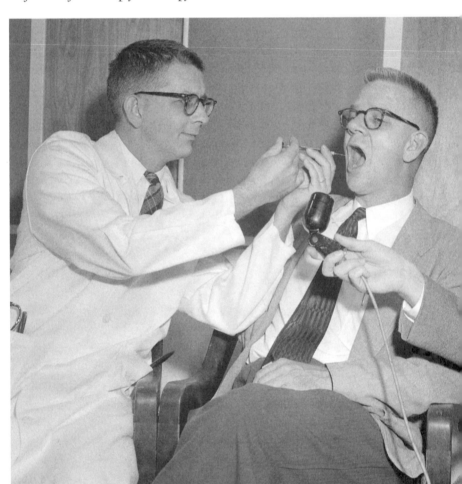

In the first half of the twentieth century, doctors treated some cases of depression, addiction, and other mental illnesses with psychotherapy, which has fewer risks. This treatment involves a patient talking with a therapist to help solve psychological or behavioral problems. Patients are encouraged to recall childhood memories and explore their subconscious thoughts and feelings in order to uncover the sources of their problems. This approach, however, can take weeks, months, or years to produce results.

Since the late 1940s psychiatrists have had great expectations for the usefulness of LSD in psychotherapy. Researcher Leigh A. Henderson summed up the psychiatric community's goals for LSD this way:

> LSD was expected to shorten the lengthy and expensive process of psychotherapy; it would enable patients to recall the childhood experiences and unconscious material that often did not emerge for months or years in

The International Federation of Internal Freedom conducts a group therapy experiment in 1963 with subjects under the influence of LSD.

conventional psychotherapy. LSD was a drug that would effect fundamental changes in attitudes and personality, not just a reduction in the outward symptoms of mental illness. It was expected to be of particular value in patients who were resistant to more conventional therapies.[58]

Two primary approaches emerged for using LSD therapy. Psycholytic therapy used small doses (approximately 50 micrograms) of LSD in a series of sessions. This type of therapy was used in addition to normal psychotherapy. Psycholytic therapy was primarily used in Europe and was thought to help loosen the mind and remove blocks that kept patients from responding to standard psychotherapy. Therapists also believed that the use of LSD helped patients recall childhood memories and explore their subconscious.

The second approach is called psychedelic therapy and involved high doses (up to approximately 250 micrograms) of LSD. Practiced primarily in the United States, psychedelic therapy was designed to be used only a few times and to cause a profound psychological experience. Therapists believed that the experience would be so intense that it would cause a permanent change in the patient's personality and thought processes, leading to a type of conversion to a new life. Researcher Dr. Stanislav Grof thought that psychedelic therapy probably produced an "ecstatic state" with "feelings of unity with other people, nature, the entire universe and God."[59] Overall, researchers believed that patients would become less depressed, anxious, guilty, and angry and, at the same time, more self-tolerant and aware.

Criticism of LSD Therapy

Because LSD's effects are powerful and difficult to control even in a medical setting, many in the medical community took, and continue to take, a strong stance against LSD therapy, saying it is too dangerous. According to pioneering LSD researcher Dr. Oscar Janiger, who began studying LSD in the 1950s, doctors did not learn how to control the unpredictable nature of the drug:

> LSD didn't pan out as an acceptable therapeutic drug for one reason. Researchers didn't realize the explosive nature of the drug. You can't

manipulate it as skillfully as you would like. It's like atomic energy—it's relatively easy to make a bomb, but much harder to safely drive an engine and make light. And with LSD we didn't have the chance to experiment and fully establish how to make it do positive, useful things.[60]

Critics of LSD therapy continue to believe that the potential risks of LSD therapy far outweigh the benefits. They say that nothing good could result from a drug that could potentially cause mental problems such as delirium or psychoses. Noting that LSD and other hallucinogens have long-term consequences in healthy people, Dr. Gregory Collins, an alcohol- and drug-recovery expert, commented, "I would be reluctant to try them in the mentally ill."[61]

LSD and Safety in Research

In an effort to answer concerns about the short-term and long-term safety of LSD research, a follow-up study of LSD experiments conducted by Janiger from 1954 to 1962 was funded by the Multidisciplinary Association for Psychedelic Studies (MAPS). The organization has a membership of 1,600, including many prominent research scientists. According to Harvard-trained social scientist and founder of MAPS, Rick Doblin, Janiger's early research was important because it focused on the effects of LSD in relatively healthy people who were not psychiatric patients. This meant that the results of the experiments could be attributed to LSD, not to illness.

The follow-up study included interviews with forty-five of the people who participated in Janiger's studies. The average age of these people at the time of their interviews was over seventy. The MAPS-sponsored study found that relatively few short-term adverse effects, such as loss of identity, were associated with Janiger's research. The study report, published in 1999, noted:

In approximately five interviews, adverse effects were reported during the LSD experiences, even though these experiences were considered, on balance, positive. These adverse effects ranged from having physical pain to a temporary loss of identity to psychological discomfort with a perceived inhospitable set and setting. In each case, these adverse effects did not preclude these respondents from reporting that the LSD experience was, on balance, positive.[62]

The Greatest Misconception About LSD

Dr. Stanislav Grof explored the use of LSD as a therapy at the Psychiatric Research Institute in Prague until the mid-1960s and then at Johns Hopkins University until 1973. He worked closely with LSD and conducted more than four thousand sessions of psychedelic therapy. When asked by interviewer Jerry Snider what he thought the greatest misconception about LSD was, Grof replied:

> I would say these two reactions reflect the basic misconception, that LSD is either good or bad. It is neither. By itself, LSD has no intrinsic healing potential, nor does it have any intrinsic destructive potential. The outcome depends on who is doing it, with whom, for what purpose and under what circumstances. Yet everything that happens under the influence of LSD tends to be credited or blamed on the drug itself.

> Years ago . . . I had a very interesting discussion with Humphrey Osmond, one of the early pioneers of LSD research. He pointed out . . . that LSD is just a tool. He said if the worth of some other tool, a knife for instance, was discussed in the same way LSD was, you'd have a policeman saying it was bad, while pushing statistics of people killed with knives in back alleys. A surgeon would see it as good, pointing out the healing possibilities of the knife. A housewife might talk about cutting salami. An artist might talk about woodcarving. As you can see, what is being said says less about the knife than about how it is used. We don't make the mistake of blaming or crediting the knife with how it's used, but with LSD it's all kind of thrown together.

One person from the past studies did experience mildly disturbing flashbacks that lasted from six months to one year. The study authors noted that previous study reviews of LSD patients conducted in 1960, 1971, and 1984 also reported relatively few adverse persistent symptoms.

The Effectiveness of LSD Therapy Remains Unknown

Although most of Janiger's healthy research subjects had positive experiences, the majority reported that they did not think there were any long-lasting benefits. Only a few said they thought the experience had long-term positive effects, such as providing a more positive outlook on life. In contrast, results of LSD psycholytic

Despite extensive testing, the effectiveness of LSD as a complement to psychotherapy has not been determined.

therapy research from 1988 to 1993 by the Swiss Medical Society for Psycholytic Therapy were more positive.

Unlike the healthy patients in Janiger's study, some of the patients (38 percent) in the Swiss study were diagnosed with personality disorder. This disorder is characterized by a set of traits that combine to negatively affect a person's life and may include poor self-image, inability to have good relationships with other people, and impulsive behavior. Many patients also had adjustment disorders, in which a person trying to adjust to a stressful event experiences depression and anxiety. The final major disorder that patients in the study suffered from were affective disorders, such as manic depression.

In 1994 and 1995, a follow-up study was conducted of 171 patients who participated in the Swiss study. Overall, nine out of ten of the patients reported to have good or slight improvement concerning their psychiatric problems. In interviews with the patients, 46.3 percent of them reported good improvement following psycholytic treatment, and 38.8 percent reported a slight improvement in their condition. No change in their condition was reported by 5.8 percent in the study, and 4.2 percent reported that they felt their condition had worsened.

According to the author of the follow-up report, Dr. Peter Gasser, the Swiss study still does not prove that the psycholytic therapy was effective. He noted that to prove effectiveness, new and better designed studies would have to be made. For example, this study did not compare the results of patients treated with LSD to those of control groups or to those of patients who had received different kinds of treatments or no drugs at all. Such comparisons are important because they provide evidence that it was the LSD producing the effects and not some other factor, such as patients' expectations that the drug would cure them. Dr. Gasser said, "A different study design would be needed to obtain more persuasive evidence of efficacy. Such a design would require testing subjects before and after treatment, and randomly assigning subjects to treatment and control groups."[63]

Flaws in Research

In fact, reviews of LSD research have shown that many of the early studies had serious flaws compared to studies using current research standards. In the early studies researchers usually knew who was taking LSD, which could influence their judgment concerning how effective the results were. For example, if the researchers already believed the drug worked, they might be more likely to interpret results as being positive in the patients who took LSD. Many of the researchers did not define in clear terms exactly how the patients improved. For example, in evaluating alcoholic patients, they would need to define factors such as how long the patients stayed off of alcohol or how much they reduced their consumption. Because of these flaws, critics said that it was uncertain whether or not LSD was the primary factor in bringing about improvements in patients.

According to Dr. Harrison Pope, a psychiatrist and professor at Harvard University who is interested in LSD's effects on anxiety, scientists hoping to pursue human research with LSD have to be careful. In an ABC News article, Pope noted, "It is essential that any studies in this area be performed with the most rigorous modern methods and great care to have an impartial approach."[64] For example, when Pope proposed a study of LSD-assisted therapy to reduce fear and anxiety in dying patients, he said that some patients would be given a placebo, that is, a pill that has no effect on the person taking it. This approach allows researchers to more fairly evaluate the results of their study.

Summing up the debate over research involving LSD and other hallucinogens, Pope noted, "The challenge is to design the study in such a way, that if the drug shows benefits, skeptics are convinced, and if it doesn't help, proponents of hallucinogenic use don't challenge the research as inadequate."[65]

LSD, Alcoholism, and Addiction

A small number of scientists in the United States, including Dr. Pope, are seeking to re-establish LSD research to prove whether or not it can be effective in helping some patients. One of these scientists, Dr. Richard Yensen, has served on the faculties of Harvard Medical School and Johns Hopkins University and conducted government-approved LSD experiments in Maryland in the 1970s. He is trying once again to get government approval to study LSD-assisted psychotherapy with substance abusers. Yensen has designed his proposed studies to comply with today's rigorous research standards.

Yensen says that past research with alcoholics and heroin addicts shows that LSD has potential to help treat substance abusers. For example, psychiatrists and psychologists typically used LSD therapy to provide alcoholic patients with an emotional awakening, or "peak experience," which would help convert patients to sobriety. In *LSD Psychotherapy*, author W.V. Caldwell defined the LSD peak experience as "a religious sense of at-oneness, a resurgence of faith and hope, and a radiant affirmation of the value of life."[66]

LSD and the CIA

The psychiatric profession was not the only group interested in researching LSD. The U.S. Central Intelligence Agency (CIA) was looking for a speech-inducing drug that it could use as a type of truth serum on suspected foreign agents. Over three decades, the CIA conducted more than four hundred experiments with LSD in U.S. and Canadian hospitals, prisons, universities, and military installations and at their own safe houses in Washington, New York, and San Francisco.

Although research indicated that LSD was an unreliable truth serum, the CIA thought that the military could possibly use LSD against an entire population to produce temporary mass hysteria or uncontrollable fear. As noted by Tad Szule in a 1977 *Psychology Today* article, "The CIA's Electric Kool-Aid Acid Test," the CIA once reported, "The lysergic-acid derivative can produce a temporary state of severe imbalance, hysteria, insanity. . . . Conceivably, this might be an unusually merciful agent of warfare: temporarily nullifying the individual's effectiveness, but not permanently damaging him."

The CIA's experiments, conducted under the names ARTICHOKE and Project MK-Ultra, took a wrong turn when a forty-three-year-old civilian biochemist employed by the Army Medical Corps committed suicide nine days after taking the drug. The man jumped out of a hotel window in New York City, where he had been taken for treatment after becoming depressed following his LSD use.

The CIA temporarily halted further experimentation but soon began to study the drug again. When CIA inspector general John Earman discovered the secret testing program in 1966, he recommended halting the tests. They were deemed unethical and phased out over the next decade.

Yensen has noted that he believes the peak experience can give addicts the determination they need to stop using drugs or alcohol. According to Yensen and his colleague Dr. Donna Dryer, a review of early studies has shown that 53 percent of patients receiving high-dose psychedelic therapy reported that they quit using alcohol, compared to 33 percent who received low-dose therapy. Only 12 percent who had conventional therapy with no LSD reported quitting.

Perhaps the most impressive of the early research were two Canadian studies by Dr. S.E. Jensen published in 1963. These studies showed a 75 percent improvement in alcoholic patients

LSD, the Doctor-Patient Relationship, and Dying

Dr. Richard Yensen, who began studying LSD in the 1970s, believes that LSD-assisted therapy could have many benefits. But he also says that the drug is not a cure-all. In fact, he does not even think the drug itself is the key to success in most types of LSD-assisted therapy. According to Yensen, LSD therapy that is practiced correctly harkens back to an older era of medicine in which the doctor-patient relationship was emphasized:

> The doctor-patient relationship is the key to successful treatments incorporating LSD. There are as many relationships as there are doctors and patients. If the relationship is not good the likelihood for a negative or difficult experience is high. If the relationship is good, even if the experience is difficult, the person is likely to derive benefit from it.

Yensen also says his past research indicates that LSD-assisted therapy and a good doctor-patient relationship allow patients to work through the idea of dying and explore in depth the way they think about death. Yensen noted in a 2004 interview with the author:

> We're talking about an opportunity to examine ideas, to examine where the person came to feel the way they feel about death or life or themselves. And, when they can do that and break through to positive experiences of a mystical sort, their entire picture improves—fear of death diminishes, their zest for living increases, their requirements for pain medication decreases. Whether they say they are in objectively less pain or the same pain as before, they require less medicine because they basically want to be alive and alert for the whole process of dying. Their orientation shifts towards what they can give to the living and away from so much focus on the sadness of their plight.

after they received a single large dose of LSD. An important aspect of Jensen's studies was that they addressed some of the criticisms concerning LSD therapy and research. In *LSD—The Problem-Solving Psychedelic*, authors P.G. Stafford and B.H. Golightly, noting the objections about inadequate testing procedures, said, "Dr. S.E. Jensen of the Saskatchewan Hospital, Weyburn, reported an excellent controlled experiment dealing with some of the most difficult cases." They added,

> One group of alcoholics was put in the hands of psychiatrists who did not use LSD. Another group was prepared for LSD treatment, but not given

it, while a third group—after identical preparation—was given the drug. The criteria for "much improved" were stiff: "complete abstinence at the time of the follow-up."[67]

However, some scientists point out that the patients in this study may have improved on their own or as a result of other components of the treatment program.

LSD and Dying

Another area of interest is LSD-assisted psychotherapy in the treatment of depression and anxiety in cancer patients. Early LSD

Some practitioners have found LSD to be a useful tool in therapy for terminally ill patients suffering from depression and anxiety.

research reported good results using LSD to help people who were suffering from a painful terminal illness. In fact, the results of using LSD to help with pain and fear were so promising that studies in this area by Richard Yensen and others were among the last to be discontinued in the early 1980s.

One of the early pioneers of this research was Dr. Eric C. Kast. In 1964 he published a series of reports through the American Medical Association on the administration of LSD to more than 150 patients who were dying, primarily from cancer. Kast noted that LSD was as effective as other drugs in relieving pain and that the effects lasted much longer, even after the LSD trip was over. Furthermore many of the patients were better able to deal with the pain after it returned. As noted by Kast, freedom from pain lasted ninety-two hours with 100 micrograms of LSD as compared to two or three hours with painkilling narcotics. Several other studies obtained similar results.

Kast and others did question the morality of interfering with the very personal process of dying. In his last study of 128 people, seven said that they resented the use of LSD because it changed their concepts of life and death. The majority, however, said they were gratified and had gained deeper insights into life and death. Kast noted, "In human terms, the short but profound impact of LSD on the dying was impressive."[68]

A New Era in LSD Research

In addition to pursuing the use of LSD in therapy, scientists are currently conducting new avenues of investigation. Researchers interested in studying LSD note that science has greatly advanced over the past several decades and provides a new and better understanding of the brain's neurochemistry and how it affects human thought, emotions, and behavior. They believe that observing the effects of LSD on the brain can give them insight into human behavior and mental illness. Writing in a 1994 National Institute on Drug Abuse report, Dr. Stephen Szara, who was chief of the institute's biomedical research branch at the time, stated, "Recent advances in the neurosciences and cognitive sciences have

Huxley, LSD, and Dying

Renowned author Aldous Huxley, who wrote *Brave New World*, among many other works, was profoundly interested in the phenomenon of dying and in the religious and mystical experiences induced by drugs like LSD. Huxley, like some LSD researchers, believed that LSD and other hallucinogens could help people better understand and accept death as well as deal with its pain. When Huxley was dying of cancer in 1963, he asked his wife, Laura, to give him 100 micrograms of LSD. She later described Huxley's final dying moments while under the influence of LSD in her book *This Timeless Moment:*

> The twitching [of Huxley's lower lip] stopped, the breathing became slower and slower, and there was absolutely not the slightest indication of contraction, of struggle. It was just that the breathing became slower—and slower—and slower; the ceasing of life was not a drama at all, but like a piece of music just finishing so gently . . . and at five twenty the breathing stopped.

In the book, Laura Huxley also noted, "Aldous died as he lived, doing his best to develop fully in himself one of the essentials he recommended to others: Awareness."

created opportunities for using hallucinogens as tools in attacking the supreme mystery: How does the brain work?"[69]

LSD and the Brain

Some researchers believe that new medical technology and advances in molecular biology combined with LSD studies can provide insights into how the brain functions. These insights may lead to the development of new medications for a variety of problems. One area of research focuses on the neurotransmitter serotonin, which LSD is known to affect.

Serotonin plays a role in human emotions and mental health, as well as the functioning of various body systems, such as the cardiovascular system. By studying how LSD affects serotonin, scientists believe that they can gain a better understanding of serotonin function, which could lead to new therapies for mental problems such as depression, anxiety, panic disorder, and obsessive-compulsive disorder. It could also lead to treatments and better care for other

Timothy Leary interviews Laura Huxley, widow of author Aldous Huxley, in 1996. Laura administered LSD to her dying husband at his request.

problems like heart disease and even migraine headaches. According to Dr. David E. Nichols, founder of the Heffter Research Institute, "While no one would suggest that LSD will be useful as a tool to study every aspect of serotonin function, the fact remains that it has been an important fundamental tool and catalyst in helping to understand the roles that serotonin plays in the brain."[70]

Another area of LSD research focuses on the brain's genetic response to the drug. Genes are the fundamental building blocks of life, and they control the many different chemical functions of the body. By studying LSD's effects on genes in the brain, scientists hope to learn more about human behavior and certain brain functions. Such studies may possibly lead to better diagnosis of behavioral or mental problems, including addictions, eating disorders, and depression. They could also lead to the discovery of new drugs to treat behavioral problems or help improve brain functions such as memory and learning.

Dr. Charles D. Nichols is conducting genetic studies of the brain using LSD. He has found that LSD affects genes in the prefrontal cortex of rats. Located in the front of the brain, the prefrontal cortex is involved in planning, thinking, learning, memory, judging, personality, and social behavior.

Specifically, Nichols has found that LSD affects genes that regulate synapses. Synapses are gaps between brain cells (neurons) that allow information to pass between them in the form of chemical neurotransmitters, such as serotonin. The brain responds to stimuli by adjusting how much information is communicated between neurons. The brain also changes the physical pattern of these connections between neurons, including forming new synapses and eliminating or altering old synapses. LSD studies of synapses may help scientists better understand how the brain modifies itself, adapts to experience, learns, and remembers.

Human Study

Although animal experiments with LSD are being conducted, the debate continues as to whether researchers should be allowed to administer LSD to humans. LSD cannot be used in therapy, and research on people requires a special license from the federal government. The government remains reluctant to grant permission for human study. For example, Richard Yensen initially received approval to conduct his studies with LSD, but the government decided to put the project on hold. Yensen and others are calling for the FDA and others to allow tightly controlled and regulated human studies using LSD.

Scientists and the medical community agree that the potential for abuse of the drug remains and that there are dangers to consider. Dr. George Greer, a psychiatrist and medical director of the Heffter Research Institute, has noted, "If hallucinogens ever find their way into mainstream medicine—and I am convinced they will—they will never be handed out like Prozac. People will need guidance. These are not drugs you administer every day."[71]

Whether or not research into LSD will progress further and prove or disprove the drug's effectiveness in some areas of psychiatric

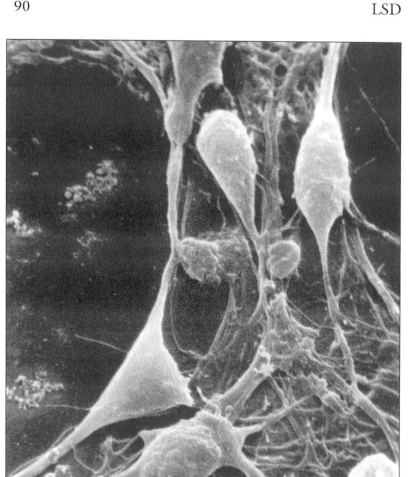

A micrograph image of neurons in the human brain. Some studies show that LSD positively affects the genes that regulate the synapses between neurons.

treatment is still undetermined. As long as LSD is manufactured and used illegally, the drug will remain a major concern for the government and the general public.

Notes

Introduction: A Different and Mysterious Drug

1. Quoted in Judy Monroe, "The LSD Story," *Current Health*, April–May 1998, p. 24.
2. Leigh A. Henderson and William J. Glass, eds., *LSD: Still with Us After All These Years*. San Francisco: Jossey-Bass, 1994, p. 3.
3. Drug Enforcement Administration (DEA), "LSD in the United States," ca. 1995. www.fas.org.
4. Monroe, "The LSD Story," p. 24.

Chapter 1: LSD's Origins

5. Albert Hofmann, *LSD: My Problem Child*. New York: McGraw-Hill, 1980.
6. DEA, "LSD in the United States."
7. K.H. Blacker, et al., "Chronic Users of LSD: The 'Acid-heads,'" *American Journal of Psychiatry*, September 3, 1968.
8. Edward M. Breecher and the editors of *Consumer Reports, The Consumers Union Report on Licit and Illicit Drugs*. New York: Little, Brown, 1972. www.drugtext.org.
9. B. Kent Houston, "Review of the Evidence and Qualifications Regarding the Effects of Hallucinogenic Drugs on Chromosomes and Embryos, *American Journal of Psychiatry*, August 2, 1969, pp. 252–254.

Chapter 2: LSD and the Mind

10. Leonard Gibson, "The LSD Experience: A Whiteheadian Interpretation," *Process Studies*, Summer 1977, pp. 97–107.
11. Leigh A. Henderson, "About LSD," in *LSD: Still with Us After All These Years*, p. 45.

12. Albert Rosenfeld, Barry Farrell, and the editors of *Life*, "A Remarkable Mind Drug Suddenly Spells Danger LSD," *Life*, March 25, 1966. www.psychedelic-library.org.
13. DEA, "LSD in the United States."
14. Henderson, "About LSD," p. 46.
15. Henderson, "About LSD," p. 46.
16. William Braden, *The Private Sea, LSD and the Search for God.* Chicago: Quadrangle, 1967. www.druglibrary.org.
17. Braden, *The Private Sea.*
18. Timothy Leary, Ralph Metzner, and Richard Alpert, *The Psychedelic Experience.* www.erowid.org.
19. Canadian Government Comission of Inquiry, "LSD," 1972. www.druglibrary.org.
20. R.J. Strassman, "Adverse Reactions to Psychedelic Drugs: A Review in the Literature," *Journal of Nervous and Mental Diseases,* October 1984, pp. 577–595.
21. James MacDonald and Michael Agar, "What Is a Trip— and Why Take One?" in *LSD: Still with Us After All These Years,* p. 18.
22. Henderson, "Adverse Reactions," in *LSD: Still with Us After All These Years,* p. 69.
23. DEA, "LSD in the United States."
24. American Academy of Child and Adolescent Psychiatry, "Psychosis," 2001. www.aacap.org.
25. Canadian Government Commission, "LSD."
26. Henderson, "Adverse Reactions," in *LSD: Still with Us After All These Years,* p. 64.
27. Henderson, "Adverse Reactions," in *LSD: Still with Us After All These Years,* p. 73.

Chapter 3: LSD Use: Yesterday and Today

28. Breecher et al., *Consumers Union Report.*
29. Breecher et al., *Consumers Union Report.*
30. Quoted in Rosenfeld, Farrell, and the editors of *Life*, "A Remarkable Mind Drug."

31. Linda Bayer, *Strange Visions: Hallucinogen-Related Disorders*. Philadelphia: Chelsea House, 2000, p. 31.
32. Lester Grinspoon and James B. Bakalar, *Psychedelic Drugs Reconsidered*. New York: Basic, 1979. www.psychedelic-library.org.
33. Grinspoon and Bakalar, *Psychedelic Drugs Reconsidered*.
34. Grinspoon and Bakalar, *Psychedelic Drugs Reconsidered*.
35. Timothy Leary and Richard Alpert, "Foreword," in Alan Watts, *The Joyous Cosmology*. New York: Random House, 1962. www.druglibrary.org.
36. Quoted in Doctors for Life, "Testimonies of Ex-Drug Addicts," www.dfl.org.za.
37. Quoted in MacDonald and Agar, "What Is a Trip—and Why Take One?" in *LSD: Still with Us After All These Years*, p. 14.
38. Quoted in University of Michigan, News and Information Services, "Rise in Ecstasy Use Among American Teens Begins to Slow," December 19, 2001. http://monitoringthe future.org.
39. Quoted in University of Michigan, "Rise in Ecstasy Use."
40. Quoted in U.S. Department of Health and Human Services, "Teen Drug Abuse Declines Across Wide Front," December 19, 2003. www.hhs.gov.
41. Quoted in Health and Human Services, "Teen Drug Abuse Declines."

Chapter 4: LSD and the Law

42. Quoted in Michael Montagne, "From Problem Child to Wonder Child: LSD Turns 50," *Bulletin of the Multidisciplinary Association for Psychedelic Studies (MAPS)*, Spring 1993. www.maps.org.
43. Rosenfeld, Farrell, and the editors of *Life*, "A Remarkable Mind Drug Suddenly Spells Danger."
44. Quoted in Richard Yensen and Donna Dryer, "Rediscovering a Lost Psychedelic Therapy," *Shared Vision*, July 2000. www.shared-vision.com.

45. Quoted in S. Szara, "The Hallucinogenic Drugs—Curse or Blessing?," *American Journal of Psychiatry*, June 1967, p. 1517.
46. DEA, "Controlled Substances Act." www.usdoj.gov.
47. DEA, "LSD in the United States."
48. Quoted in PBS, *Frontline*, "Drug Wars," interview with Bill Alden. www.pbs.org.
49. Quoted in Ellen Perlman, "Terms of Imprisonment," *Governing*, April 2000. www.governing.com.
50. Families Against Mandatory Minimums, "Mandatory Sentencing Was Once America's Law-and-Order Panacea. Here's Why It's Not Working." www.famm.org.
51. Harriet Ryan, "Mandatory Minimums: Fair or Foul?," Courtroom Television Network, 2002. www.courttv.com.
52. Office of National Drug Control Policy, News and Public Affairs, "White House Drug Czar Testifies Before House Appropriations Subcommittee on Success, Future of National Drug Control Efforts and the National Youth Anti-Drug Media Campaign," April 9, 2003. www.whitehouse drugpolicy.gov.
53. John P. Walters, "The President's National Drug Control Strategy, To the Congress of the United States," March 2004. www.whitehousedrugpolicy.gov.
54. Correctional Association of New York, "Effective Alternatives to the Drug Laws: What Works Best for Nonviolent Drug Offenders," February 2001. www.droptherock.org.
55. Quoted in Shawn Zeller, "Education Against Drugs," *The Harvard University Gazette*, February 20, 1997. www. news.harvard.edu.
56. Correctional Association of New York, "Effective Alternatives to the Drug Laws."
57. Quoted in PBS, *Frontline*, "Drug Wars."

Chapter 5: LSD in Research

58. Quoted in Henderson, "About LSD," p. 47.

59. Quoted in Stanislav Grof, *LSD Psychotherapy*, 2nd ed. Alameda, CA: Hunter House, 1994.

60. Quoted in John Whalen, "The Trip," *LA Weekly*, July 3–9, 1998. www.laweekly.com.

61. Quoted in Robert Eisner, "Medical Hallucinogens?," ABCNEWS.com, March 22, 2001. www.abcnews.go.com.

62. Quoted in Rick Doblin, Jerome E. Beck, Kate Chapman, and Maureen Alioto, "Dr. Oscar Janiger's Pioneering LSD Research: A Forty Year Follow-Up," *Bulletin of the Multidisciplinary Association for Psychedelic Studies, MAPS*, Spring 1999, pp. 7–21.

63. Quoted in Peter Gasser, "Psycholytic Therapy with MDMA and LSD in Switzerland," *Bulletin of the Multidisciplinary Association for Psychedelic Studies, MAPS*, Winter 1994–1995, pp. 3–7. http://maps.org.

64. Quoted in Eisner, "Medical Hallucinogens?"

65. Quoted in Eisner, "Medical Hallucinogens?"

66. Quoted in P.G. Stafford and B.H. Golightly, *LSD—The Problem-Solving Psychedelic*. New York: Award, 1967. www.druglibrary.org.

67. Quoted in Gasser, "Psycholytic Therapy."

68. Quoted in Richard Leiby, "The Magical Mystery Cure," *Esquire*, September 1, 1997. www.lycaeum.org/forums.

69. Quoted in Paula Kurtzweil, "Medical Possibilities for Psychedelic Drugs," *FDA Consumer Magazine*, September 1995. www.fda.gov.

70. David E. Nichols, "A Scientist Reflects on the Discovery and Future of LSD," 1995. www.heffter.org.

71. Quoted in Sandra Blakeslee, "Scientists Test Hallucinogens for Mental Ills," *New York Times*, March 13, 2001. www.maps.org.

Organizations
to Contact

Drug Enforcement Administration
Mailstop: AXS, 2401 Jefferson Davis Highway
Alexandria, VA 22301
(202) 307-8846
www.usdoj.gov
This is the Department of Justice organization dedicated to enforcing the controlled substances laws and regulations of the United States.

Drug Policy Alliance
70 West 36th Street, 16th Floor, New York, NY 10018
(212) 613-8020
www.drugpolicy.org/homepage.cfm
Drug Policy Alliance is the leading organization working to broaden the public debate on drug policy based on science, compassion, health, and human rights.

Erowid
P.O. Box 1116, Grass Valley, CA, 95945
www.erowid.org
Erowid.org is an online library of information about psychoactive plants and chemicals and related topics. It provides a compilation of the experiences and efforts of hundreds of individuals, includ-

ing users, parents, health professionals, doctors, therapists, chemists, researchers, teachers, and lawyers.

Multidisciplinary Association for Psychedelic Studies (MAPS)
2105 Robinson Avenue, Sarasota, FL 34232
(924) 941-6277
www.maps.org

This is a nonprofit research and educational organization that assists scientists to design, fund, obtain approval for, and report on studies into the risks and benefits of psychedelic drugs such as LSD.

National Clearinghouse for Alcohol and Drug Information
P.O. Box 2345, Rockville, MD 20847
(800) 729-6686
www.health.org

This is the branch of the U.S. Department of Health and Human Services dedicated to substance abuse prevention and treatment.

National Institute on Drug Abuse
National Institutes of Health
6001 Executive Boulevard, Room 5213
Bethesda, MD 20892-9561
(301) 443-1124
www.nida.nih.gov

The National Institutes of Health organization is dedicated to researching drug abuse and addiction.

For Further Reading

Books

Linda Bayer, *Strange Visions: Hallucinogen-Related Disorders*. Philadelphia: Chelsea House, 2000. This book describes the history and effects of LSD and other hallucinogens.

Sean Connolly, *Just the Facts: LSD*. Chicago: Heinemann Library, 2000. Young adult literature focusing on basic facts of LSD.

Martin A. Lee and Bruce Shlain, *Acid Dreams: The Complete Social History of LSD: The CIA, the Sixties, and Beyond*. New York: Grove Weidenfeld, 1992. The authors, both noted journalists, provide a colorful but accurate in-depth look at the events that shaped how LSD is viewed by society.

Robert Masters, Jean Houston, and Robert E.L. Masters, *The Varieties of Psychedelic Experience: The Classic Guide to the Effects of LSD on the Human Psyche*. Rochester, VT: Park Street, 2000. This book provides a detailed account of the psychedelic experience.

Web Sites

Heffter Research Institute (www.heffter.org). This site contains the latest information on LSD and other hallucinogen research.

Psychedelic Library (www.druglibrary.org). This Web site contains past and current information on LSD.

Works Consulted

Books

Edward M. Breecher and the editors of *Consumer Reports, The Consumers Union Report on Licit and Illicit Drugs.* New York: Little, Brown, 1972. This early report includes discussions about LSD use by the general public and in research.

Gerald G. Briggs, ed., *Drugs in Pregnancy and Lactation: A Reference Guide to Fetal and Neonatal Risk.* Philadelphia: Lippincott Williams & Wilkins, 2001. Provides information useful to doctors and pregnant women about the possible adverse effects of various drugs on a developing fetus.

Marlene Dobkin de Rios and Oscar Janiger, *LSD, Spirituality, and the Creative Process.* Rochester, VT: Park Street, 2003. Based on the results of one of the longest clinical studies of LSD that took place between 1954 and 1962, the book focuses on an exploration of how LSD influences imagination and the creative process.

Lester Grinspoon and James B. Bakalar, *Psychedelic Drugs Reconsidered.* New York: Basic, 1979. A comprehensive survey of psychedelic drugs and related issues.

Stanislav Grof, *LSD Psychotherapy.* 2nd ed. Alameda, CA: Hunter House, 1994. An in-depth review of LSD's use in psychotherapy.

Leigh A. Henderson and William J. Glass, eds., *LSD: Still with Us After All These Years.* San Francisco: Jossey-Bass, 1994. Offers insights for parents, counselors, and educators as to why young people use LSD.

Albert Hofmann, *LSD: My Problem Child*. New York: McGraw-Hill, 1980. Provides an overview of LSD's scientific and social history, as well as the discoverer's personal views about the drug.

Steven B. Karch, ed., *Drug Abuse Handbook*. San Francisco: CRC, 1997. A handbook for professionals who deal with problems related to drug abuse. Discusses workplace drug testing, drug crime, addiction medicine, and overdoses.

Richard R. Laing, ed., *Hallucinogens: A Forensic Drug Handbook*. San Francisco: Academic, 2002. A highly technical book for anyone who investigates or prosecutes cases involving hallucinogens.

Andrew Weil, *The Natural Mind*. Boston: Houghton Mifflin, 1986. A book on the principles of human consciousness with some discussion of LSD.

Periodicals

K.H. Blacker et al., "Chronic Users of LSD: The 'Acidheads,'" *American Journal of Psychiatry*, September 3, 1968.

Rick Doblin, Jerome E. Beck, Kate Chapman, and Maureen Alioto, "Dr. Oscar Janiger's Pioneering LSD Research: A Forty Year Follow-up," *Bulletin of the Multidisciplinary Association for Psychedelic Studies, MAPS*, Spring 1999.

Leonard Gibson, "The LSD Experience: A Whiteheadian Interpretation," *Process Studies*, Summer 1977.

B. Kent Houston, "Review of the Evidence and Qualifications Regarding the Effects of Hallucinogenic Drugs on Chromosomes and Embryos," *American Journal of Psychiatry*, August 2, 1969.

J.C. Klock et al., "Coma, Hyperthermia, and Bleeding Associated with Massive LSD Overdose, A Report of Eight Cases," *Clinical Toxicology*, 1975.

Judy Monroe, "The LSD Story," *Current Health*, April–May, 1998.

R.J. Strassman, "Adverse Reactions to Psychedelic Drugs: A Review of the Literature," *Journal of Nervous and Mental Diseases*, October 1984.

S. Szara, "The Hallucinogenic Drugs—Curse or Blessing?" *American Journal of Psychiatry*, June 1967.

Tad Szule, "The CIA's Electric Kool-Aid Acid Test," *Psychology Today*, November 1977.

Internet Sources

American Academy of Child and Adolescent Psychiatry, "Psychosis," 2001. www.aacap.org.

Sandra Blakeslee, "Scientists Test Hallucinogens for Mental Ills," *New York Times*, March 13, 2001. www.maps.org.

William Braden, *The Private Sea, LSD, and the Search for God.* Chicago: Quadrangle, 1967. www.druglibrary.org.

Canadian Government Commission of Inquiry, "LSD," 1972. www.druglibrary.org.

Correctional Association of New York, "Effective Alternatives to the Drug Laws: What Works Best for Nonviolent Drug Offenders," February 2001. www.droptherock.org.

Doctors for Life, "Testimonies of Ex-Drug Addicts," www.dfl.org.za.

Drug Enforcement Administration, "Controlled Substances Act." www.usdoj.gov.

———, "LSD in the United States," ca. 1995. www.fas.org.

———, "Lysergic Acid Diethylamide (LSD)," February 2004. www.usdoj.gov.

———, "Pickard and Apperson Sentenced on LSD Charges: Largest LSD Lab Seizure in History," November 25, 2003. www.usdoj.gov.

Robert Eisner, "Medical Hallucinogens?" ABCNEWS.com, March 22, 2001. www.abcnews.go.com.

Families Against Mandatory Minimums, "Mandatory Sentencing Was Once America's Law-and-Order Panacea. Here's Why It's Not Working." www.famm.org.

Peter Gasser, "Psycholytic Therapy with MDMA and LSD in Switzerland," *Bulletin of the Multidisciplinary Association for Psychedelic Studies, MAPS*, Winter 1994–1995. http://maps.org.

Dana Hunt, "Rise of Hallucinogen Use," Washington, DC: National Institute of Justice, October 1997. www.abtassoc.com.

Laura Huxley, *This Timeless Moment.* New York: Farrar, Straus, & Giroux, 1968. Reprinted on The Passage from Life to Death, "Excerpt from 'O Nobly Born!'" www.maps.org.

Paula Kurtzweil, "Medical Possibilities for Psychedelic Drugs," *FDA Consumer Magazine*, September 1995. www.fda.gov.

Timothy Leary and Richard Alpert, "Foreword," in Alan Watts, *The Joyous Cosmology.* New York: Random House, 1962. www.druglibrary.org.

Timothy Leary, Ralph Metzner, and Richard Alpert, *The Psychedelic Experience.* www.erowid.org.

Richard Leiby, "The Magical Mystery Cure," *Esquire*, September 1, 1997. www.lycaeum.org.

Michael Montagne, "From Problem Child to Wonder Child: LSD Turns 50," *Bulletin of the Multidisciplinary Association for Psychedelic Studies, MAPS*, Spring 1993. www.maps.org.

National Institute on Drug Abuse, "Hallucinogens and Dissociative Drugs," National Institute on Drug Abuse Research Report Series, March 2001. http://165.112.78.61/PDF/RR Halluc.pdf.

David E. Nichols, "A Scientist Reflects on the Discovery and Future of LSD," 1995. www.heffter.org.

Office of National Drug Control Policy, "Early Intervention Initiative," January 29, 2004. www.mediacampaign.org.

——, News and Public Affairs, "White House Drug Czar Testifies Before House Appropriations Subcommittee on Success, Future of National Drug Control Efforts and the National Youth Anti-Drug Media Campaign," April 9, 2003. www.whitehousedrugpolicy.gov.

PBS, *Frontline*, "Drug Wars," interview with Bill Alden. www.pbs.org.

Ellen Perlman, "Terms of Imprisonment," *Governing*, April 2000. www.governing.com.

Paul Perry, "LSD Psychosis," 1996. www.vh.org.

Albert Rosenfeld, Barry Farrell, and the editors of *Life*, "A Remarkable Mind Drug Suddenly Spells Danger LSD," *Life*, March 25, 1966. www. psychedelic-library.org.

Harriet Ryan, "Mandatory Minimums: Fair or Foul?" Courtroom Television Network, 2002. www.courttv.com.

Jerry Snider, "Has Psychology Failed the Acid Test? Stanislav Grof," www.lightparty.com.

P.G. Stafford and B.H. Golightly, *LSD—The Problem-Solving Psychedelic*. New York: Award, 1967. www.druglibrary.org.

University of Michigan, News and Information Services, "Rise in Ecstasy Use Among American Teens Begins to Slow," December 19, 2001. http://monitoringthefuture.org.

U.S. Department of Health and Human Services, "Teen Drug Abuse Declines Across Wide Front," December 19, 2003. www.hhs.gov.

U.S. Department of Justice, Office of Justice Programs, "Rise in Hallucinogen Use," October 1997. www.serendipity.li.

John P. Walters, "The President's National Drug Control Strategy, to the Congress of the United States," March 2004. www.whitehousedrugpolicy.gov.

John Whalen, "The Trip," *LA Weekly*, July 3–9, 1998. www. laweekly.com.

Richard Yensen and Donna Dryer, "Rediscovering a Lost Psychedelic Therapy," *Shared Vision*, July 2000. www.shared-vision.com.

Shawn Zeller, "Education Against Drugs," *Harvard University Gazette*, February 20, 1997. www.news.harvard.edu.

Index

Picture Credits

About the Author

David Petechuk is a freelance writer who specializes in medicine and the health sciences. He is a former director of publications for the health sciences at the University of Pittsburgh. Mr. Petechuk has worked with numerous psychiatrists throughout his career and helped coauthor a series of publications by the Department of Justice on juvenile delinquency based on the work of child psychiatrists. He is also the author of a book on the respiratory system.